W9-AKU-779

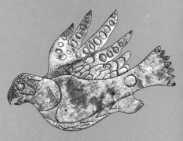

930
COR

96-73
595

930
COR   96-73

Corbishley, Mike
The ancient world

DATE DUE	BORROWER'S NAME
	David
	Robyn G-T Kim
	Scott
	Deborah G-T
	Nick G-T

CLARA BARTON LIBRARY
BORDENTOWN, NJ 08505

DEMCO

THE
ANCIENT
WORLD

Mike Corbishley

Illustrated by James Field

37599000027308

PETER BEDRICK BOOKS
NEW YORK

TIMELINK: ANCIENT WORLD ,

First American edition published in 1992 by

Peter Bedrick Books
2112 Broadway
New York, NY 10023

Copyright © Reed International Books Limited 1992

Text copyright © Mike Corbishley

Designed and produced by Lionheart Books

Published by agreement with Hamlyn Children's
Books, London, England

All rights reserved. No part of this publication may be
reproduced, stored in a retrieval system or transmitted,
in any form or by any means, electronic, mechanical,
photocopying, recording or otherwise, without the prior
written permission of Peter Bedrick Books.

Library of Congress Cataloging-in-Publication Data
Corbishley, Mike.
    The ancient world : from the first people to the fall of Rome. --
1st American ed.
        Author's statement: t.p. verso.
        Includes index.
        Summary: Surveys the history of the ancient world, from prehistoric times
to the fall of the Roman Empire.
        ISBN 0-87226-354-1
        1. History, Ancient--Juvenile literature. [1. History, Ancient.] I. Title.
    D57.C78   1992
    930--dc20   92-4844   CIP   AC

Printed in Hong Kong
5 4 3 2 1

Acknowledgements
Designer: Ben White
Project Editor: Lionel Bender
Text Editor: Mike March
Picture Researcher: Jennie Karrach
Media Conversion and Typesetting:
    Peter MacDonald and Una Macnamara
Managing Editor: David Riley
All maps by Stefan Chablik.

Picture credits
Page 9: Michael Holford. Page 10: Michael Holford.
Page 15: Arlette Mellaart. Page 20: Werner Forman
Archive. Page 24: Michael Holford. Page 28: Robert
Harding. Page 36: Michael Holford. Page 42: Werner
Forman Archive. Page 44: ZEFA. Page 46: ZEFA.
Page 49: Jenny Pate/Hutchison Library.
Cover, page 1: Lionel Bender. Cover: ZEFA.

Roman engineers and
builders constructing an
aqueduct in about AD 50
– see pages 52 to 53.

CONTENTS

Left: Tuthankhamon's mask, an example of the elaborate decorative work of the ancient Egyptians – see pages 28-29.

INTRODUCTION

This book is an introduction to the greatest events in world history from the earliest humans, over four million years ago, to the end of the Roman Empire in about 450 AD. It is divided into eight chapters arranged in time sequence from the beginning of the ancient period. Within each chapter there is a general overview of world events, short features on important civilizations, kingdoms and battles, and extended features on subjects of special interest, for example the Egyptian Kingdom or the Stone Age farming settlement at Çatal Hüyük in present-day Turkey.

The Ancient World is the first volume in the Timelink series, which is designed to give young readers an overall view of different peoples and their history, and the links between civilizations across the globe. It does not cover the entire history of the ancient world, but it does show many of the significant turning points – the great events that changed the way people lived then and influenced the way we all live now.

Throughout **The Ancient World** there are many maps, illustrations, diagrams, photographs and timecharts. The maps show the migrations, or movements, of people and the spread of civilizations and empires. The illustrations show how the people dressed, what their homes looked like, and how and what they built and farmed. They include

Above: Early farmers, their livestock and houses – Skara Brae, on the island of Orkney c3100 BC.

reconstructions of villages, temples and scenes from everyday life. Timecharts list the dates of important events across the globe. At the back of the book the dates are put together in two large timecharts covering the whole of the ancient period. These are for quick, easy reference. In addition, there is a Glossary explaining some of the jargon and technical terms used in the book.

Finding out about the Ancient World

How do we know what happened hundreds or thousands of years ago? Usually we can build up a picture of everyday life in ancient times by collecting together all the evidence we have from that period and interpreting it in the same way that detectives will look for clues at the scene of a crime and try and find out "who did it, why and when".

In the vast period we call prehistory, before people made written records, the only evidence comes from objects actually left behind – clothes, weapons, tombs, paintings, for example. We call all these objects archaeological evidence. Historians, who study and write about the past, use this information and can also read and interpret written records to try to work out what sort of lives people led. In this book, you can study that evidence, in words and pictures, and make up your own mind about the effect of the great events in ancient history.

UNDERSTANDING DATES

Ancient peoples used several types of calendar, which is a way of dividing up the year into months and of arranging the years in some sort of order. Today, in the developed world, we use a calendar based on that developed by the ancient Romans more than 2,000 years ago. It is based on the date of the birth of Jesus Christ as the starting point. Events occurring before that date are counted backwards from it – Before Christ, or BC for short. So the dates given for a person who lived before Christ will read, say, 250-191 BC. The first date is the person's year of birth and the last date is the time of their death. Events happening after the birth of Christ are counted forwards from it. They are given the letters AD, from the Latin words anno domini, meaning in the year of the Lord. A famous person's dates written as AD 191-250 show that they were born 191 years after the birth of Christ and died 59 years later, when the calendar indicated 250 years had passed since Jesus Christ was born.

All the dates given in this book are based on the BC and AD system. However, because of the uncertainty of ancient history and the problems of converting dates from one type of calendar system to another, it has not always been possible to be precise. Then, the abbreviation c for the Latin word circa, meaning about, is used before the date. For the same reasons, you may find that other history books give slightly different dates from this book for the same events. Some give Jesus Christ's birth year as around 4 BC and not AD 1.

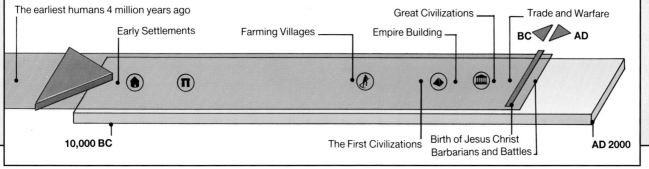

The earliest humans 4 million years ago

Early Settlements

Farming Villages

Empire Building

Great Civilizations

Trade and Warfare

BC / AD

10,000 BC

The First Civilizations

Birth of Jesus Christ
Barbarians and Battles

AD 2000

THE CHANGING WORLD

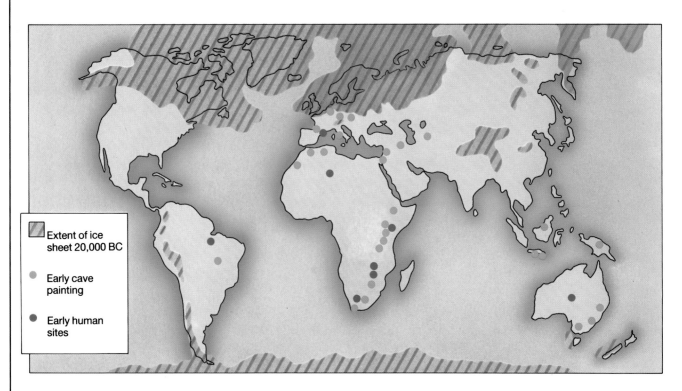

Extent of ice
sheet 20,000 BC

Early cave
painting

Early human
sites

⊙ SPREAD OF PEOPLES 4 MILLION TO 10,000 BC

Archaeologists have discovered recently that the ancestors
of humans today inhabited parts of the Earth as long as 4
million years ago. Gradually these hunters and food-
gatherers spread into every continent. In some areas
nomadic peoples created paintings and carvings.

⊙ EARLY CIVILIZATIONS 10,000 TO 4000 BC

In about 10,000 BC the great ice sheets began to melt. The
hunting peoples discovered how to farm animals and crops.
This meant that they settled and produced wealth.
Civilizations could be established – the Near East was the
first area to see cities and complex societies.

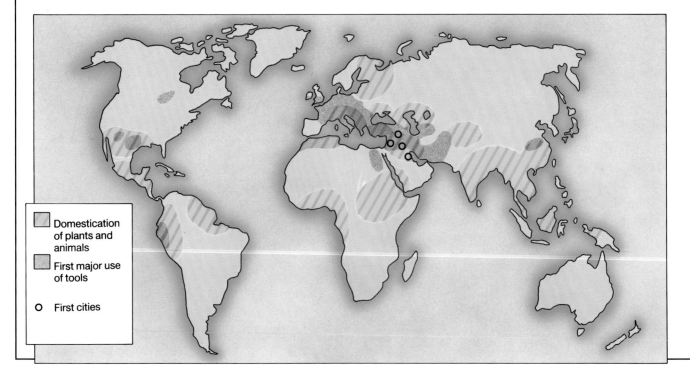

Domestication
of plants and
animals

First major use
of tools

O   First cities

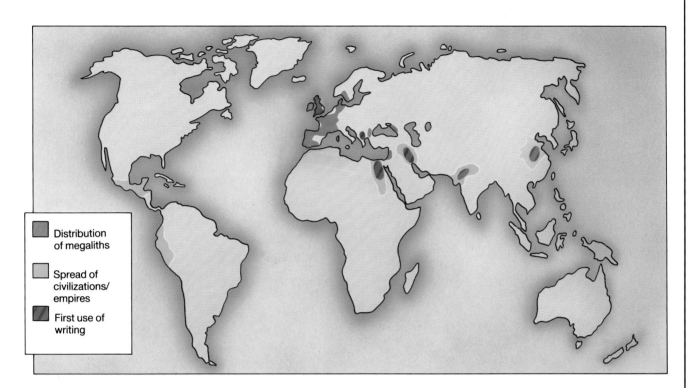

Legend:
- Distribution of megaliths
- Spread of civilizations/empires
- First use of writing

Ⓐ EMPIRE BUILDING 4000 TO 1000 BC

Some of the early civilizations grew into empires, taking over lands around them. At first this development was centered on the Mediterranean Sea. Later, other empires were established in Asia and the Americas. Empires soon began to make contact with, and go to war with, other empires.

⒱ CLASH OF EMPIRES 1000 BC TO AD 450

In this period two empires were the most important – Greece and Rome. They came into conflict with each other. Rome became the dominant force in the Mediterranean, the Near East, North Africa and Europe. The Romans clashed with some eastern empires but had trading links with the Far East.

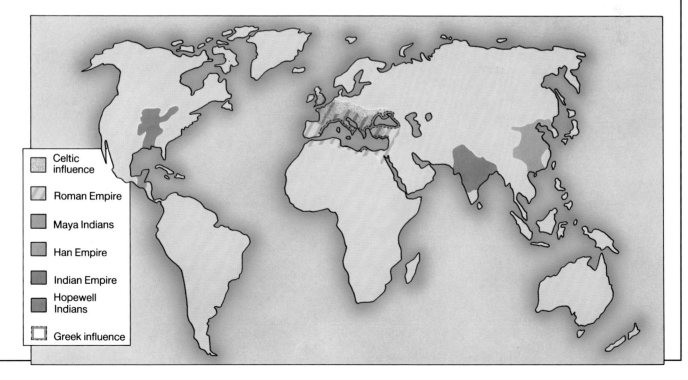

Legend:
- Celtic influence
- Roman Empire
- Maya Indians
- Han Empire
- Indian Empire
- Hopewell Indians
- Greek influence

THE FIRST PEOPLES

Human beings are closely related to the great apes (chimpanzees, orang-utans and gorillas) which still exist in some parts of the world. Both seem to have evolved from the same ancestor millions of years ago. But evidence from this period is difficult to find – and there is not much of it.

The tree of the past

Sometimes people draw up a 'family tree', which shows who their relatives and ancestors are. Drawing up a tree of the family of early human beings is more difficult, as there are few definite links. Somewhere between 10 million and 4 million years ago a type of hominid (early human being) called *Australopithecus* developed. The name means 'southern ape'.

Anthropologists (scientists who study the remains of ancient peoples and the lives and customs of modern peoples) are not certain whether these early hominids were the direct ancestors of modern human beings. Another type of early human, called *Homo*, was found from about 2.5 million years ago. *Homo habilis* and *Homo erectus* were living at

THE FIRST HUMANS

Australopithecus afarensis

Australopithecus africanus

Australopithecus robustus

Homo habilis

Homo erectus

Neanderthalensis

Homo sapiens

⊙ HUMAN ORIGINS

Early hunters had to know a lot about their environment, and to understand the plants and animals that they needed to live on. They also had to be skilled in making tools from flint, or other stone, and organic materials such as wood, bone or leather. One skill, being practiced here, was hardening a wooden spear by charring the end in a fire. Much later, the hunters of Jericho or Star Carr (see page 11) would have made tools and weapons in this way.

△ Only the bones (sometimes fossilized) of these early people have been discovered. From reconstruction of the skeletons, artists have shown what the people may have looked like. By about 40,000 years ago most of the world was populated by modern humans (see below).

MODERN HUMANS – Early hunter-gatherers

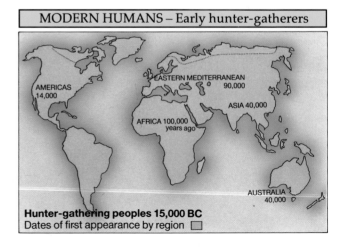

AMERICAS
14,000

EASTERN MEDITERRANEAN
90,000

ASIA 40,000

AFRICA 100,000
years ago

AUSTRALIA
40,000

Hunter-gathering peoples 15,000 BC
Dates of first appearance by region ☐

Early Stone Age tool

△ The very first tools were made by striking pieces off lumps of flint, like this chopping and scraping tool from near Lascaux (see below).

A 'hand-axe'

the same time as the *Australopithecus* hominids. Remains of *Homo erectus* have been discovered in Kenya, Africa. This early type of human has also been found outside Africa, in China and other parts of East Asia.

There were other types of our own species, *Homo sapiens*. One of the earliest types was called *Homo sapiens neanderthalensis*. These people lived in Europe from about 400,000 to 200,000 years ago. They were intelligent hunters who buried their dead. The earliest evidence we have of *Homo sapiens sapiens* – modern humans – is from 100,000 years ago.

ⓐ OLDUVAI GORGE

Olduvai Gorge in Tanzania is one of the most famous places in the history of humans because the first examples of both *Homo habilis* and a type of *Australopithecus* were discovered there. Pre-humans and early humans were living at Olduvai Gorge from about 1.7 million years ago. At that time the weather was wetter than today and there was a lake there. Both these early human types were nomadic hunters who traveled long distances in pursuit of animals and foraged for other food. At Olduvai, and at other sites in East Africa, stone tools have been found: simple choppers and skilfully made 'hand-axes', all-purpose cutting tools.

ⓥ LASCAUX

Some of the first modern humans (*Homo sapiens sapiens*), who were hunter-gatherers, produced some remarkable art – cave-paintings, carvings and statues – about 35,000 years ago. This art must have been part of rituals connected with hunting and fertility. Probably the most famous examples are the cave-paintings at Lascaux in south-western France. A large number of paintings were made on the walls of the cave in about 15,000 BC. They include paintings of animals such as horses, bison, cows, stags and ibexes. This tells us that the climate of France was warmer then than it is today, and that many wild animals roamed the countryside.

Cave painting at Lascaux

Hunter at Laetoli

ⓥ LAETOLI

Evidence for a group of hominids, *Australopithecus afarensis*, dated to about 3.4 million years ago, has come from Laetoli, in Ethiopia. The evidence was in the form of the fossil remains of bones and footprints preserved in the fossilized mud. The remains of a number of individuals were found but the most complete were those of a woman. Some people believe that she was an early form of *Homo*.

EARLY SETTLEMENTS

By about 10,000 years ago the ice that had covered much of the Earth's land mass had melted. The new, warmer climate created a new environment with different animals and plants. Hunting and farming developed differently in different continents. Much depended on where people lived and what the climate there was like. The local geography and climate produced the animals that people hunted and the plants that they gathered and later cultivated.

African hunters and herders

While Europe was covered in icy glaciers from 20,000 to 10,000 BC, the Sahara region of Africa was even drier than it is today – no one could live there. By 9000 BC wildlife, such as elephants and rhinos, were living in a wetter climate. Hunters moved into the area and, finding plenty of food, began to settle. By 7000 BC there were settlements along rivers and beside lakes. People hunted, fished and, by about 6000 BC, were herding cattle and cultivating cereal crops.

ⓐ JERICHO

In an oasis in the River Jordan Valley, in the Middle East, lie the ruins of one of the earliest farming settlements in history – Jericho. People were living here from about 9000 BC onwards. The warm climate and permanent water supply meant that crops could be cultivated easily. By 8000 BC Jericho covered about 4 acres and its houses were surrounded by a strong stone wall with a tower. The people grew wheat and barley, hunted some animals, like gazelle, but also kept domesticated animals for meat and milk.

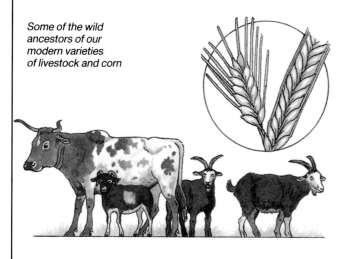

Some of the wild ancestors of our modern varieties of livestock and corn

△ The first farm animals and plants were wild. The wild ancestors of wheat were einkorn and emmer. The wild mouflon sheep was chosen to tame and breed because it gave lots of milk and meat and was not too aggressive. The bezoar goat and wild ox were probably the early ancestors of the domesticated goats and cattle around today.

▽ The area where farming first began in the world is called the Fertile Crescent. Here hunting peoples first learned to domesticate and tame both wild crops and animals. The first crops to be cultivated were wheat and barley. The first animal to be tamed was the sheep.

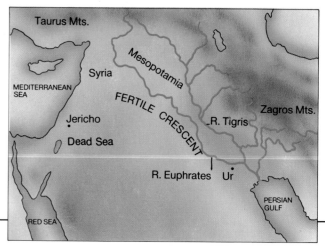

Hunters at Star Carr

▼ LEPINSKI VIR

▲ STAR CARR

As peoples in the Near East and the Mediterranean areas were beginning to farm, others in Europe were establishing permanent settlements even though they lived by hunting and gathering their food. At Lepinski Vir, on the River Danube in Yugoslavia, a settlement of wooden houses for about 100 people was built around 6000 BC. It looks as if a chief family organized this village because one of the houses is bigger than the rest and in front of it is a square or meeting place. The villagers gathered plant food, fished for carp and catfish and hunted wild cattle, deer and wild boar.

Around 7500 BC in Yorkshire, northern Britain, at a place called Star Carr, there used to be a great lake close to the coastline. Each year groups of hunters came from the high moors around to set up camp. They built huts out of wood and reeds. Archaeologists have found stone axes and arrowheads, bone and antler harpoons and the wooden paddle of a boat. Also found was part of a stag's antler with holes cut in it so that it could be attached to someone's head, as shown. Perhaps this was to attract the hunters' prey or was part of some hunting ritual.

Lepinski Vir

10,000 – 7000 BC	7000 – 5000 BC
10,000 Hunting camps in Sahara region after last Ice Age. **10,000** Settlements in Palestine – known as the Natufian culture. **10,000** Ice sheets melt in North America. Hunter camps. **9000** First wheat harvested in Syria. First sheep domesticated in Mesopotamia. **8500** First rock art in Sahara region. **8500** First cultivation of wild grasses and beans in Peru. **8300** Glaciers retreat in Europe. **8000** First true farming community in Jericho. **8000** End of Ice Age in Far East. **7000** Wheat and barley cultivated in Anatolia, pig domesticated.	**7000** Semi-permanent settlements in North America. **6500** Domesticated cattle in Africa. **6500** First farmers in the Balkans. **6500** Britain separated from mainland Europe by melting of ice. **6300** Grain and potato cultivation in Peru. **6200** Farming villages in western Mediterranean. **6000** Wheat and barley cultivated in north-eastern Africa. Farming established in northern Mesopotamia. First farming villages in China. **6000** Settlements on the great rivers of Europe. **5000** Irrigation in Mesopotamia. **5000** Rice farming in China.

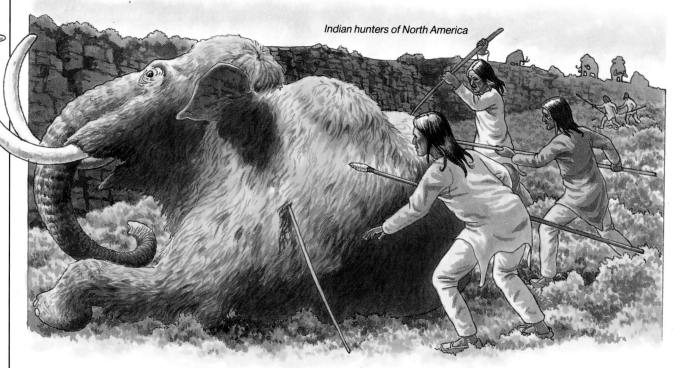

Indian hunters of North America

Europe, America and Asia

Meanwhile, in Europe, hunting and food-gathering continued until farming was introduced into the Mediterranean areas from the Near East around 6200 BC. Now that the last Ice Age had come to an end, hunters stalked smaller animals, such as deer and elk. Communities of hunters and food-gatherers now began to settle in villages.

Other parts of the world developed in different ways. We now know that hunters reached North America 14,000 years ago, crossing what was then land from Siberia. The earliest human hunters had arrived in Australia by about 40,000 years ago, traveling from either China or South-East Asia.

The agricultural revolution

The discovery that certain plants could be cultivated and certain animals could be tamed and bred for food transformed the way people lived. All this happened in the Near East. The lands that produced this 'revolution', from the Red Sea to the Persian Gulf, were called the Fertile Crescent because

⬥ HUNTERS OF WYOMING

There were hunting peoples in North America from about 12,000 BC. Having crossed the land bridge from Siberia while it was still frozen with ice, they gradually moved south, making temporary camps. These people are now known as Palaeo-Indians. Those above, of about 9000 BC, are trying to kill a mammoth. They attack it with stone-tipped spears and drive it into a ravine, where it is killed and cut up. Other animals hunted at this time were bison, tapirs and horses. From about 7000 BC the American hunters gatherered more plant foods and began to establish semi-permanent villages wherever they found good supplies of wild crops and water.

AFRICA
10,000 Hunters move into Sahara region. **8500** Hunters develop small flint weapons. **8300** First rock art in the Sahara region. **7500** First pottery made in Sahara region. **6500** First domesticated cattle in Africa. **6000** Wheat and barley first cultivated in north-eastern Africa. Millet cultivated in Sahara region. Wheat, barley and sheep introduced to Egypt from Near East.

EUROPE
8300 Glaciers retreat. Small flint weapons developed. **8000** Hunters move into Lappland. **6500** First farmers in the Balkans. Wheat, barley, sheep and goats introduced from Anatolia. **6200** Farming villages in western Mediterranean. **5200** Farming spreads westwards and reaches Netherlands. **5000** Gold and copper worked into objects in the Balkans.

Houses and storage pots at Banpo

STONE TOOLS AND POTTERY

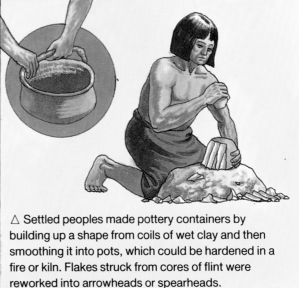

△ Settled peoples made pottery containers by building up a shape from coils of wet clay and then smoothing it into pots, which could be hardened in a fire or kiln. Flakes struck from cores of flint were reworked into arrowheads or spearheads.

⊛ BANPO VILLAGE, CHINA

The end of the last Ice Age, about 10,000 years ago, produced changes in the environment all over the world. In some parts of China, Japan and Korea there were good supplies of animals, fish, shellfish and wild plants for the people to hunt and gather. They established semi-permanent settlements. From around 6000 BC farming peoples lived in small villages, like this one at Banpo, near the River Zhuan in northern China. The houses were round, built of wood and had daub-plastered walls. The whole village was surrounded by a ditch. The people grew crops such as millet, cabbage, plums and hazelnuts and kept pigs and dogs.

ASIA	AMERICA, FAR EAST
10,000 Natufian settlements in Palestine. **9000** Wheat harvested in Syria, sheep domesticated in Mesopotamia. **8000** First true farming community at Jericho. **7000** Wheat, barley, pigs and goats farmed in Anatolia. Çatal Hüyük founded. **6500** Earliest discovered textiles manufactured at Çatal Hüyük. **6000** Farming established in northern Mesopotamia.	**10,000** First peoples reach southern tip of Americas. **8500** Wild grasses and beans cultivated in Peru. **8000** End of Ice Age in Far East. **7000** First crops cultivated in Mexico. **7000** First cultivation of root crops in New Guinea. **6000** First farming villages in China. **5000** Maize cultivated in Mexico. Some farming in Amazon region. **5000** Rice farming in China.

of their shape. The wet climate at the end of the ice ages, around 10,000 BC, produced woodlands and wild grasses. These grasses were cultivated to produce our modern cereal crops – wheat and barley.

At first people in the Fertile Crescent herded gazelles and wild goats. Gradually they began to tame the goats and then to breed them for food. Other animals were domesticated and became farm animals later – sheep first, approximately 9000 BC in Mesopotamia, then pigs around 7000 BC in Turkey, and cattle around 6000 BC in northern Africa and the lands around the Aegean Sea.

Settlements, villages and towns

The production of food from crops and animals yielded a surplus, which the people could store away or use to trade with other peoples. Settlements of hunters who carried on some farming gradually grew bigger and became rich villages such as Jericho. In the Near East some villages, such as Çatal Hüyük (see page 14), became small towns.

13

ÇATAL HÜYÜK

Close to the Taurus Mountains, in what is now Turkey, is Çatal Hüyük – site of one of the largest and busiest villages of the first farmers in the world. The village was founded around 7000 BC. By 6000 BC it had grown into a town with a population of about 6,000 people. The town was gradually added to and rebuilt until it became a distinct mound (called a *tell*) by around 5720 BC. The site was excavated in 1961.

Farming and trade

The people of Çatal Hüyük grew a variety of food. Their main crops were wheat, barley and peas, but they also grew beans, fruit and nuts. They tamed wild cattle and also caught wild sheep. They were hunters – particularly of deer and wild boar – but did not rely on hunting for their main source of food. Çatal Hüyük became a prosperous town by becoming a center for trade in the Anatolian region. Its skilful craftspeople produced pottery, flint and stone tools and weapons, and copper jewelery.

Town houses

The houses in Çatal Hüyük were all joined together. There were no streets and no front doors! You entered the houses through the roof by ladders. Inside, each house had one

ÇATAL HÜYÜK

16,000 Konya Lake dries up, leaving a fertile plain for early farmers.
7000 Wheat and barley first cultivated and the pig domesticated in region of Çatal Hüyük.
Foundation of Çatal Hüyük settlement below the volcanoes of Hasan Dag and and Karaca Dag. Hunting supplements farming. Tools of obsidian (volcanic glass), flint and copper. Farming by irrigation introduced.
6200 Copper smelted at Çatal Hüyük
6000 Çatal Hüyük now a prosperous town of about 6,000 people.
6000 Farming properly established in northern Mesopotamia.
5720 Town, now rebuilt many times, exists as a mound on the landscape.

▷ The site of Çatal Hüyük is in the Konya Plain of Turkey, some 50 miles north of the Taurus Mts. Until about 16,000 BC the plain had been a lake. When it dried out it left a fertile soil for the farmers of Çatal Hüyük to cultivate.

TURKEY

● Çatal Hüyük

Taurus Mountains

MEDITERRANEAN SEA

CYPRUS

Fertile Crescent

big room (about 16 by 13 feet) with raised areas, perhaps for sleeping on.

In among the houses the archaeologists found a number of buildings that had been used for worship and ceremonies. One goddess in particular was worshipped in a room where the skulls of bulls had been carefully plastered and painted, and on the walls were paintings in red of vultures attacking headless human corpses.

Obsidian tools

◁ The people of Çatal Hüyük used their local glass (called obsidian) to make tools and ornaments.

▽ This wall painting in a shrine at Çatal Hüyük gives us a ground plan of houses below an erupting volcano – probably the nearby Hasan Dag.

◁ The houses at Çatal Hüyük each had a main room with raised benches for sleeping and eating, a hearth and a bread oven. Some of the dead of each family were buried under these raised platforms. Generally, people only lived till their early thirties.

15

FARMING VILLAGES

Prehistoric peoples had to survive in environments that were often hostile to them. The early farmers at Skara Brae (see page 18) had to build themselves storm-proof houses. The farmers of the Russian steppes also learned to cope with severe climates (see page 19). Communities of people from as far apart as Africa and northern Europe either survived as hunters or learned how to farm and to build villages, and then towns.

Hunters of Australia

The Aborigines of Australia developed an extraordinary ability to survive in surroundings in which food was hard to come by. By 25,000 years ago there were many settlements of hunters in Australia. Besides hunting animals such as the kangaroo, they also collected and ate whatever they could find.

5000 – 3500 BC
5000 Irrigation in Mesopotamia.
5000 Gold and copper worked into objects in the Balkans.
4500 Farming established around River Ganges, India.
4500 Boats with sails first used in Mesopotamia. Cattle used to pull ploughs.
4500 Megalithic tombs in western Europe.
4000 Flint mined for tools and weapons in western Europe.
4000 Millet and sorghum cultivated in the Sudan.
4000-3000 Inuits (Eskimos) move into Asia from America.
3800 First defended villages in Europe.
3650 First wheeled vehicle burials in southern Russia.

3500 – 3000 BC
3500 Cotton cultivated and textiles made in Peru.
3500 Simple plows first used in northern and western Europe.
3500 First civilizations established in Sumeria.
3400 First defended towns in Egypt.
3250 Earliest writing in the world, in Mesopotamia.
3200 Maize cultivated in South America.
3200 Circles of megalithic stones in Britain and northern France.
3100 Cuneiform writing used in Mesopotamia. Long-distance trade with Syria.
c.3050 First Pharaoh of Egypt, Narmer.
3000 First farming evidence in Korea.
3000 Hieroglyphic writing in Egypt.

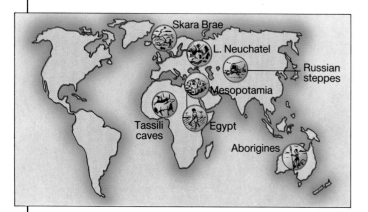

◁ The first farming communities developed in the Middle East, Europe and northern Africa while peoples in the Americas and Australia were still living as hunter-gatherers.

The location of Tassili

Tassili caves in N Africa

▶ THE PAINTINGS OF TASSILI

In 6000 BC the Saharan region of Africa had a climate which was much wetter than it is today. The rain produced a variety of plants which animals could live on. The hunting peoples used rock shelters in the mountains, such as those in the Hoggar Mountains, as camping places. On the walls of these shelters the hunters drew pictures of animals and themselves. At first, around 8500 BC, they painted only wild animals – rhinoceros, elephant, giraffe and hippopotamus. Then, from 6000 BC, there were paintings like this, showing that the people of Tassili had tamed cattle and were driving their herds from place to place to find new grazing land.

This included oysters, eggs, moths, honey, grubs and roots. They knew how to manage their environment and sometimes they re-planted wild crops. The difficult climate, with its long periods of drought, prevented the growing of crops on a larger scale. This did not encourage permanent settlements.

However, they had an ordered society, with religious ceremonies and the burial of their dead (from as early as 25,000 years ago). There were artists in their communities, painting cave walls and decorating objects like necklaces of shells. Some Aborigines still manage to live their traditional lives today.

The spread of farming villages
Within the birthplace of farming – the Fertile Crescent (see page 10) – the main area of farming villages was northern Mesopotamia.

⊽ UBAID HOUSES – MESOPOTAMIA

From about 5500 to 4000 BC people were building houses like this in villages and small towns in southern Mesopotamia. Archaeologists have been able to identify different types of settlement from the pottery they found there. This house is from the Ubaid period about 4500 BC. Its walls have been made from mud-bricks left to harden in the sun. The bricks were then plastered over. Floors and roof too were covered with plaster. Each house had its own hall and living rooms and an outside courtyard.

⊽ EGYPT BEFORE THE PHARAOHS

Egypt was a good place to live if you were a hunter-gatherer. The climate and the River Nile produced plenty of animals and plants to eat. By 5000 BC there were villages of farmers in the Nile valley. The flooding of the Nile each year irrigated and spread fertile mud on to the fields. Irrigation channels were cut to carry the precious water inland from the Nile to fields, gardens and orchards. Vegetables were grown, as well as corn, and flax to be spun into linen. Much of the land was worked by hand. The farmworkers used hoes, hand ploughs and spades made of wood. These early Egyptians had some metal, but it was rare. Flint was still used for knife blades and arrowheads and for sickles to cut the crops. The Nile was also a source of building material. River-bank clay was molded into bricks and dried in the sun.

Early Egyptian farmers

Farming settlement at Skara Brae

⊙ SKARA BRAE

These are the houses of farming families who lived on the island of Orkney off the north coast of Britain. The place is called Skara Brae today. In 3100 BC there was a small village here of about six houses, all joined together by covered passageways. The houses were stone-built – they even had stone cupboards, beds and water-containers. The village was beside a lake so there were plenty of fish and shellfish to eat. But the people were farmers. They left behind the bones of cattle, sheep, pigs and dogs. Skara Brae was abandoned in about 2450 BC, when the village was gradually covered by blown sand.

EUROPE

6200 Farming reaches western Mediterranean from the Fertile Crescent.
5200 Farming spreads into western and northern Europe, reaching the Netherlands by this date.
5000 Objects of copper and gold made in the Balkans.
4500 Cattle used to pull plows in central Europe. Megalithic tombs constructed in western Europe.
4000 Flint mined in northern and western Europe.

First farmers in Britain still using stone tools.
3800 Defended villages in western Europe.
3500 Simple plows first used in northern and western Europe.
3200 Circles of megalithic stones constructed in Britain and northern France (see page 27). First wheeled vehicles in Europe.
3000 Villages and towns defended by walls and ditches.

Mesopotamia means 'between the rivers', the rivers being the Tigris and Euphrates. Other areas of farming villages were around the Taurus and Zagros Mountains.

The farming peoples of northern Mesopotamia could rely on natural water sources, a hot climate and regular rainfall. This enabled them to grow crops all year round. They grew wheat and barley and kept animals such as goats, sheep, cattle and pigs. Archaeologists have found the bones of wild animals such as the gazelle, and so we know the people were also still hunting for food.

Further south in Mesopotamia the people who lived nearer the Persian Gulf did not have enough rainfall for their crops. However, they developed irrigation techniques, channelling the regular spring floods caused by the Rivers Tigris and Euphrates to water their fields. Canals were dug to divert water to where needed, as early as 5000 BC.

More crops produced by better farming techniques meant that villages became both bigger and wealthier. The villagers built granaries in which to store their crops. Small towns now grew up. Eridu, in southern Mesopotamia, had a population of about 4,000 people in 4000 BC. Soon places like Eridu would become the sites of the first 'civilizations'.

Lakeside houses
on stilts

Grave in the
Russian steppes

◉ LAKE NEUCHATEL VILLAGE

The earliest farmers built villages to fit into their
surroundings. In several parts of northern Europe villages
were built on the edges of lakes. This one is on Lake
Neuchatel in Switzerland at about 3800 BC. The houses
were on stilts to protect the inhabitants from wild animals.
The water provided a means of communication with other
villages. The villagers' main source of food was from farming
crops and domesticated animals but they also hunted and
used the lake for fishing. Because the village was built over
the lake's edge the remains of the houses have been
preserved. Archaeologists have also found remains of seeds
from farm crops, fruits and nuts.

◉ RUSSIAN STEPPES

The Russian steppes were not ideal lands for early farmers.
The climate of hot summers and very cold winters made it
difficult to grow the varied crops people grew in the Near
East. But there were plenty of grasslands, and animals were
bred from about 4500 BC. The areas occupied by these
farmers were around the Black Sea and the Aral Sea and
around the Altai Mountains in Siberia. At this time the
commonest animal, used for both food and transport, was
the horse. The farmers also bred sheep, goats and pigs.
Four-wheeled wagons were used and have been found in
graves, like this one, from about 3650 BC. Such burial
places belonged to people who had been rich or important.

THE AMERICAS

5000 Maize, beans,
squash, chilli peppers first
cultivated in Mexico.
Small-scale cultivation in
the Amazon region.
Bottle gourd grown as a
container introduced into
North America.
4000 First pottery in the
Americas produced in the
Amazon region.
3500 Llama first used as a
pack animal in Peru.
Cotton cultivated and
used to make textiles and
fishing nets in Peru.
3200 Maize first cultivated
in South America.
3114 First date in the
Mayan calendar.
3000 First villages in the
Tehuacan valley, Mexico.

AFRICA

6000 First farmers in
Saharan region of Africa.
5000 Saharan region still
fertile. Crop farming and
also cattle herding.
4400 Palm trees grown as
a crop in the Sudan for oil
and nuts.
4000 Millet and sorghum
cultivated in the Sudan.
Increase in population in
Egypt, larger villages.
Boats with sails in Egypt.
3400 First walled towns in
Egypt at Naqada and
Hieraconpolis.
c.3050 First Pharaoh of
Egypt, Narmer.
3000 First evidence of
Egyptian hieroglyphic
writing.

PACIFIC

5000 Millet, cereals and
rice farming in China.
Sea-level rise in
Australasia – New Guinea
and Tasmania islands
formed.
4000 Jade stone imported
into China, used for
weapons and decorative
objects.
3000 Occupation of
coastal regions of
Australasia by hunters
and fishers. Dingo (dog)
introduced into Australia
probably from South-
East Asia. People buried
and cremated. Rock art
more common in
Australia.
First agriculture in Korea
– millet introduced from
China.

ASIA

5000 Ubaid culture in
Mesopotamia. Irrigation
increases farming crops.
4500 Farming established
around the River Ganges,
India.
Boats with sails in use in
Mesopotamia.
4400 Horse domesticated
in the Russian steppes for
riding and for meat.
3650 First vehicle burials,
in southern Russia.
3500 First civilizations
based on cities
established in Sumeria.
3250 Earliest writing in the
world (pictographs) in
Mesopotamia.
3100 Cuneiform writing
used in Mesopotamia.
Long-distance trade with
Syria.

THE DISCOVERY OF METALS

It was important for both hunting and farming peoples to find good raw materials for making tools and weapons. At first stone, especially flint, was used. By 6000 BC people had discovered that copper ore could be mined and hammered into different shapes. Gradually tools of metal replaced those made from flint. Gold was another metal which was used at this time. The first places where people made things out of copper were the Balkans (Romania, Bulgaria and Yugoslavia) and southern Spain. Later, these metalworkers began to smelt copper ore and made tools by pouring molten metal into molds.

Bronze and iron

By about 2800 BC specialists discovered that, by adding about 10 per cent of tin to copper, they could produce a much harder metal – bronze. By 2000 BC those areas of Europe, such as southern Britain and Brittany in France, which had tin deposits underground were producing fine bronze tools and weapons.

Iron occurs naturally in many parts of the world. It was being smelted in western Asia by 2000 BC, whereas in western Africa it was not in use before 500 BC. The Celtic peoples in northern Europe smelted iron into bars and used it as money.

⦿ COPPER AND GOLD

Casting metal required great skill and experience. Prehistoric peoples gradually discovered better techniques and experimented with different materials. The metalworkers here are pouring molten copper into molds to make axes and spearheads – precious objects in society that were traded widely across Europe.

⦿ BRONZE

The Shang dynasty in China (see pages 36-7) was famous for its elaborate bronze objects used in ceremonies. Here bronze is cast using the 'lost wax' method. The original object is made of wax, then surrounded by soft clay and fired in a kiln. The wax flows out, leaving a perfect cast into which molten metal can be poured.

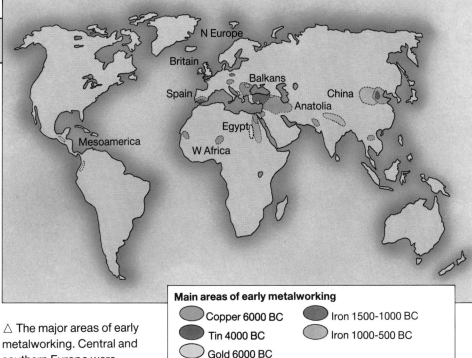

△ The major areas of early metalworking. Central and southern Europe were dominant.

Main areas of early metalworking

- Copper 6000 BC
- Tin 4000 BC
- Gold 6000 BC
- Iron 1500-1000 BC
- Iron 1000-500 BC

◁ The discovery that metal could be beaten and melted into shapes allowed better tools to be made. Various metals were discovered at different times across the world.

▽ This amphora, a storage jar for fermented mare's milk, was made by Scythian people (see page 42) in about 500 BC. Its decorated surface is a gold sheet which has been shaped around the silver base.

THE FIRST USE OF METALS

COPPER
7000-6000 Anatolian peoples.
Copper mined in Hungary, Yugoslavia and elsewhere and traded with people in Çatal Hüyük (see page 14) and others. Copper (and gold) worked by hammering into shape. Used for weapons, tools or decoration.
4000-2000 Iberian peoples of southern Spain, Egyptians and Sumerians.
1500 Mesoamericans use copper for jewelery and ornaments.

BRONZE
4000-3000 Anatolian and Sumerian peoples. Spread to rest of Asia and Europe by 2000.
2000 Bronze discovered independently in Eastern Asia.
Copper and bronze cast to make tools and weapons.

IRON
2000 Western Asia.
1500-600 Europeans, North Africa and rest of Asia.
600 Iron smelting by Chinese and cast iron by 500.
500 Western Africa, and Eastern Africa by 200.
AD 200 Southern Africa.

◀ IRON

Iron is more difficult to cast than copper or bronze because the iron ore needs to be heated with charcoal to a temperature of about 2200°F before it becomes molten. Here, in this smelting furnace in Africa around 500 BC, the ironworkers are blasting air through bellows. The slag (impurities in the metal) flows to the bottom of the furnace.

THE FIRST CIVILIZATIONS

Gradually, in different parts of the world, the small farming villages gave way to towns and to cities. They formed highly organized societies called civilizations. Some did so for reasons of war, others because of trade or population increase.

The earliest civilizations

The first civilization in the history of the world was in a country called Sumeria (present-day Iraq). Here in the land of two rivers, the Tigris and the Euphrates, the world's first cities, such as Ur (see below), were developed. But why is Sumeria called a civilization? From the objects, buildings and writings that survive, Sumeria is the first

known example of an organized society. We can see, for instance, the difference between the rich and the poor. We can identify rulers, priests, administrators and specialists. This is what made civilizations in many parts of the world, from Egypt to the Andes.

Even among those peoples who have not left us any written records, like the stone circle builders of Europe (see page 27), we can see evidence for a social class which provided rulers. These rulers may also have been priests, like those of the Indus Valley (see page 27). Egyptian kings were even treated as gods (see page 28). In each of the civilizations shown in this section, a powerful person or group controlled the society.

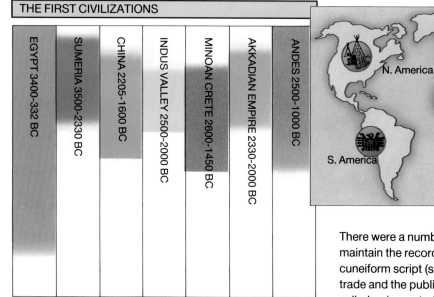

THE FIRST CIVILIZATIONS

EGYPT 3400-332 BC	SUMERIA 3500-2330 BC	CHINA 2205-1600 BC	INDUS VALLEY 2500-2000 BC	MINOAN CRETE 2600-1450 BC	AKKADIAN EMPIRE 2330-2000 BC	ANDES 2500-1000 BC

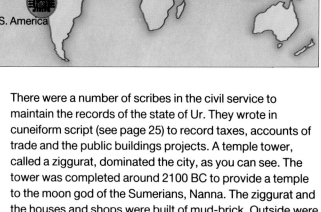

▶ UR – A CITY IN SUMERIA

One of the most important cities in Sumeria was called Ur. It started to become important in the area around 2500 BC and about 20,000 people are thought to have lived inside its walls. This was a royal city with palaces and temples as well as houses and shops which filled 60 hectares (about 130 acres). Around 2000 BC the King of Ur, Ur-Nammu, governed a large area from his cities of Ur and Uruk with an efficient civil service and a strong army.

There were a number of scribes in the civil service to maintain the records of the state of Ur. They wrote in cuneiform script (see page 25) to record taxes, accounts of trade and the public buildings projects. A temple tower, called a ziggurat, dominated the city, as you can see. The tower was completed around 2100 BC to provide a temple to the moon god of the Sumerians, Nanna. The ziggurat and the houses and shops were built of mud-brick. Outside were the rich tombs of Ur's rulers. The finest tombs were in the Royal Cemetery where kings and queens were buried not only with gold and silver ornaments but also their servants.

▷ The sacred enclosures for the temples of Ur and the ziggurat in the 115 ft. high city center.

▼ TOWNS IN THE ANDES

Along the western coast of South America villages were being expanded into towns. There were more settlements on the river valleys, where crops could be grown on hillside terraces watered by irrigation. Temple mounds, rather like the Sumerian ziggurats, were built up to 10m high. These early Peruvians had developed various art forms using fired pottery and cotton textiles.

Peruvian temple

▷ The Sumerians first used the wheel in about 3500 BC. It was an important advance for trade and for warfare. This is a model of a war chariot which would have been drawn by two wild asses.

Sumerian chariot

State organization and public buildings

In Sumeria, the Indus Valley and elsewhere city-states, as they were later called, developed. This meant that cities like Ur and Uruk in Sumeria, or Mohenjo-daro and Harappa in the Indus Valley, were small independent states. The city was the place from where the king controlled all the area round about. Sometimes the city would have a defensive wall around it. The king had administrators to help run the state. In ancient Egypt the king's official who was in charge of justice, the collecting of taxes and public works was called a vizier.

The fact that hundreds of officials were employed shows that these civilizations

3000 – 2500 BC	2500 – 2000 BC
c.3050 Foundation of Egyptian state. **3000** First evidence of agriculture in Korea. **3000** First walled strongholds, in Mediterranean Europe. **3000** Introduction of the dingo (dog) in Australia. **2920** 1st Egyptian dynasty founded. Two kingdoms united under one ruler, Menes. **2800** Villages established in Amazon region of South America. **2630** First stepped pyramid begun in Egypt. **2600** Temple mounds and religious sites in Peru. **2600** Minoan towns and palaces built. **2575** Old Kingdom Egypt. Great Pyramid of Khufu built at Giza. **2500** Trade over long distances in South America. **2500** City-states of Mesopotamia. **2500** Indus Valley cities. **2500** Large settlements in Andes region. **2500** First domesticated animals on islands in South-East Asia. **2500** North American Indian hunter-gatherers start to use campsites.	**2500** Trade links developed. Indus civilizations trade with Africa, Southern India and Mesopotamia. **2500** Walled settlements in China and first wheel-thrown pottery. **2500** Earliest woven cotton cloth found at Mohenjo-daro. **2500** First use of metals in Britain by farming peoples. **2330** Mesopotamian city-states united under Sargon I. **2300** Earliest pottery from Mesoamerica. **2205** Hsia dynasty in China. **2150** Collapse of Old Kingdom Egypt. **2040** Middle Kingdom Egypt. **2000** Large-scale cultivation of maize in Andes, South America. **2000** Amorite dynasty in Babylonia. **2000** First settlers in New Guinea. **2000** Beginning of collapse of Indus Valley civilization. **2000** Inuits (Eskimos) reach northern part of Greenland.

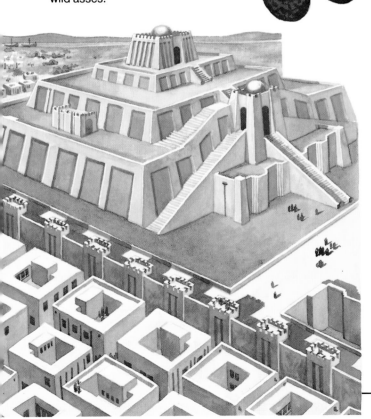

were very rich. The rulers made money by farming and exporting produce, and working people paid taxes to the state. The first civilizations, from Sumeria to South America, provide plenty of evidence as to how this extra wealth was used. In the Andes of South America great temple mounds were built (see page 23). This must have involved thousands of workers and skilled stone-cutters, all of whom would have had to be fed and perhaps paid. The people who built Stonehenge in Britain could not have been working as farmers while they were busy building. Quite possibly, some of these early societies used slave labor, but slaves too had to be fed.

⏷ MINOAN CRETE

Today we speak about King Minos of the island of Crete from the legend told by the Greeks of the beast, the Minotaur, which was half-man and half-bull. The Egyptians called Crete 'the land of Keftiu' and traded with the Cretans. The rulers of Crete grew wealthy from trade all over the Mediterranean Sea. They built themselves huge palaces, like this one at Knossos on the north coast, full of rooms, corridors and balconies set around an open court. The people of Minoan Crete worshipped gods such as the Great Earth Mother and the God of Beasts, but they must have thought the bull was sacred or important. Bulls' horns, shown in the drawing here in the Palace at Knossos, were everywhere. Knossos was destroyed in the volcanic eruption on the island of Thera 80 miles away in about 1450 BC.

Trade and specialist workers
We know that all the early civilizations traded goods; objects from each of them are widely distributed. Sometimes the goods were surplus produce. For example, Egypt was able to export some of its corn because the land was so fertile (see page 17) that it could produce more than was needed by Egypt's own people. Sometimes specialist goods were made and exported. Egypt exported papyrus for writing-scrolls, and the people of the Andes exchanged cotton textiles for colored feathers which they used as decoration and for burials.

Once each society became sophisticated enough, specialists were in great demand.

Bull's horn carvings on the steps at Knossos

▷ In the period 3000-2000 peoples moved into new territories. For example, after the fall of Ur the Amorites established the city of Babylon (see page 31) but were later overrun by the Assyrians. Trade across the Mediterranean and the Near East also brought about movements of peoples and more contact between them.

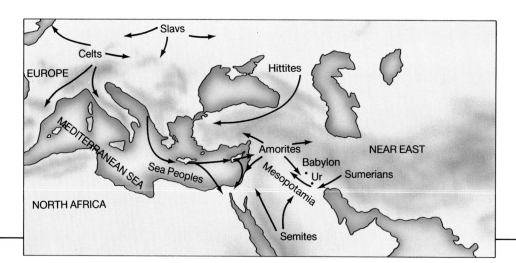

⍗ WRITING

As societies became more complex and they began to trade and collect taxes, there was a need to keep proper records. Some people, such as those of the Indus Valley, used seals to mark goods. The first proper writing was invented by the Sumerians in Mesopotamia around 3250 BC. They drew pictures of the goods that they wanted to record, such as date palms, fish or barley, on clay tablets. These 'pictograms' gradually changed into patterns, now called 'cuneiform', which stood for a sound or a syllable of a word. The Egyptians invented a different sort of writing called 'hieroglyphic' by about 3100 BC, using picture-signs. There were also two early Greek scripts. One, today called Linear A, was used by the Minoans (see opposite and below). The other, called Linear B, was developed by the Mycenaeans (see page 33). In China 'pictographs', which were simplified pictures of objects or ideas, were used from about 1500 BC.

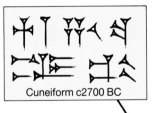

Minoan tablet

△ Tablets, like this one from Minoan Crete, were used from about 2000 BC. The seal from the Indus Valley (bottom right) has not yet been deciphered.

Cuneiform

▷ Cuneiform writing was made by pressing a wedge into wet clay. The clay was then baked into a tablet. The example shown reads 'bird', 'ox' and 'well'.

Cuneiform c2700 BC

△ The Rosetta Stone, which was found in Egypt in 1799. It was the vital clue in deciphering Egyptian hieroglyphs because the same inscription is carved in hieroglyphs, later Egyptian writing and ancient Greek (which came after Linear A and Linear B and is understood).

Egyptian scribe

▷ The Egyptian scribes used a sort of paper on which they wrote their hieroglyphic script. It was called papyrus and was made from flattened reeds.

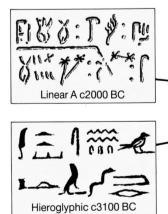

Linear A c2000 BC

Hieroglyphic c3100 BC

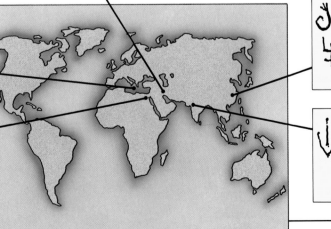

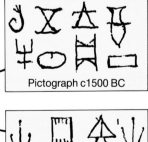

Pictograph c1500 BC

Pictogram c3000 BC

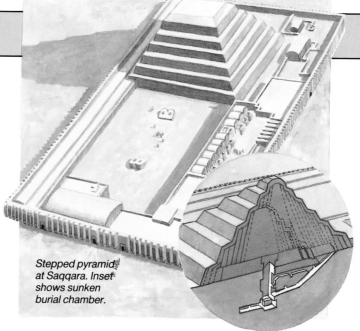

Stepped pyramid at Saqqara. Inset shows sunken burial chamber.

Clearly, there were engineers in cities like Mohenjo-daro. They devised and built the sewage- and waste-disposal systems.

In Minoan Crete (see page 24) specialist potters created massive storage jars for grain, olive oil or wine. The beautifully decorated walls of palaces like the one at Knossos show that there were skilled artists employed in Crete. In Egypt, complete communities of craftspeople were devoted to the mummification and burial of the dead.

Civilization as an idea

At one time it was thought that the idea of civilization developed in Sumeria and then spread to other parts of the world. It is much more likely, however, that the same idea arose in different parts of the world at different times as communities grew larger and more complex. There is plenty of evidence for regional differences in civilizations. For example, the Indus Valley cities had elaborate sewerage systems but there was no such thing in Minoan Crete or in South America.

ANCIENT EGYPT

The great tombs known as the Pyramids are evidence of the high level of civilization of Ancient Egypt. Even today we do not know exactly how they were built. The Great Pyramid of Cheops at Giza is one of the Seven Wonders of the Ancient World. An official called Imhotep designed the first pyramid for King Djoser in about 2630 BC. Deep underground was the burial chamber of the king. Rising 197 feet above ground was the pyramid you see here, called a stepped pyramid. It was built by a workforce of perhaps 100,000 men. Later, architects designed pyramids with smooth sides.

NEAR EAST	MEDITERRANEAN	INDIA, CHINA	THE NEW WORLD
c3100 Earliest clay tablets with pictographs from Uruk. Sumerian dynasties. Hieroglyphics in Egypt. **2750-2500** In Sumeria, larger settlements replace villages. **c2500** City-states of Mesopotamia such as Ur. Dynasty of Ur founded by Mesanepada, called 'King of Kishi'. Royal Graves at Ur. **2340** King Sargon I ruled Mesopotamia from city of Akkade. **2330** City-states around Akkade united under Sargon I. **2330-2150** Descendants of Sargon rule Akkade states. **2150** Akkade invaded by Gutian peoples (from Iran). **2050** Warfare between Sumerian states. **c2000** Amorite dynasties in Babylonia.	**Crete** **2600-2000** Early Minoan Period – harbor cities of eastern Crete and palaces. **1700** New palaces built. **1450** Eruption at Thera. End of Minoan civilization. **Greece** **2500-1600** Early and Middle Hellenic Periods. **Egypt** **c 3050** Egyptian state formed. **c 3000** Egyptian hieroglyphic writing. **c 2920** Two kingdoms united under one ruler. **2630** First pyramid begun. **2600** First 'true' pyramid built at Maidum. **2530** Great Pyramid at Giza built. **2500** Sahara begins to dry out. **2150** Collapse of Old Kingdom.	**India** **c 3500** First farmers in Indus Valley. **c 2500** First cities established in Indus Valley. **c 1900** Cities in decline. **China** **3000** Society evolving. Stone tools still in use. **2205-1766** Hsia dynasty. Yu is China's first emperor. Walled settlements and the introduction of metalworking. **1600-1027** Shang dynasty.	**Americas** **c 3200** Maize first cultivated in South America. **2500** Increase in cultivation of crops. First large settlements built in Andes region. Temple mounds built. Farming terraces and irrigation schemes. Long-distance trade. **2300** Settlements in Mesoamerica. Earliest pottery from Mesoamerica. **2000** Earliest pottery made in Andes region. Maize cultivated on a large scale. **Australasia** **2500** First domesticated animals on islands in South-East Asia. **2000** First settlers in New Guinea.

Mohenjo-daro

⦿ THE INDUS VALLEY

Along the River Indus in northern India a number of large cities were being built around 2500 BC. The largest two which have been investigated are called Mohenjo-daro and Harappa. These cities were laid out on a regular pattern. Mohenjo-daro is thought to have had a population of about 40,000. The cities had a number of stores for grain as well as palaces and religious buildings. The nearby farming areas probably paid taxes to the ruler in Mohenjo-daro in the form of produce. The whole city was equipped with a water, sewerage and rubbish-disposal system.

△ The city of Mohenjo-daro was well organized. Houses of the rich were built around a courtyard with no windows overlooking the streets. A number of single-room buildings may have been for the police.

INDUS VALLEY

c3500 First farming groups settle in Valley.
c2500 Indus civilization established. Cities of Mohenjo-daro and Harappa built. Port established at Lothol.
c1900 Indus civilization in decline. Houses neglected, irrigation works fall into disrepair.
c1500 Aryans invade northern India, coming from eastern Iran. They conquer huge areas and impose their own language by 500 BC.

⦿ FARMERS OF WESTERN EUROPE

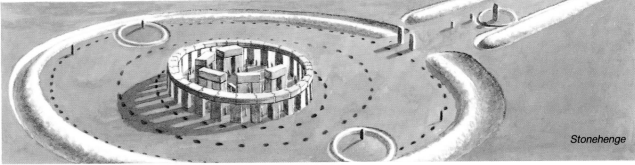

Stonehenge

The ideas and techniques of farming animals and crops gradually spread into northern and western Europe. Here societies developed differently from those further south. Although some of these farmers were rich and perhaps became the rulers, they did not build great cities. But they have left behind evidence of a unique development in

engineering skills. They built a number of monuments for religious or ceremonial rites although none as complex as Stonehenge, pictured here. By 3000 BC an area had been enclosed by a circular bank and ditch. By 2000 BC huge stones had been dragged across the surrounding plains to make a gigantic central structure.

THE KINGDOM OF EGYPT

The early hunting peoples of Egypt discovered that the soil around the River Nile was fertile enough to provide them with excellent farming land. This was because the river flooded each year, washing a layer of fertile mud on to the surrounding plains. This free fertilizer and the water were harnessed to produce fields which could grow enormous quantities of grain.

Two kingdoms of Egypt

At first the land of Egypt was governed by kings – the Kings of Upper and Lower Egypt. In about 2920 BC Egypt was united under the rule of one king. The capital city changed as different ruling families came into power. Civil servants were employed to organize and run the country and collect the taxes. The Egyptians developed complex systems of writing and record-keeping.

The rule of the Pharaohs

The title of Pharaoh, meaning 'The Great House', was given to the Egyptian king from about 1350 BC. The Pharaoh had absolute power in life and passed among the gods after death. Kings and Pharaohs had tombs built for themselves full of treasures and things to take with them into the next world. Armies of workers and artists helped to make these. The Egyptians perfected the mummification of people and animals.

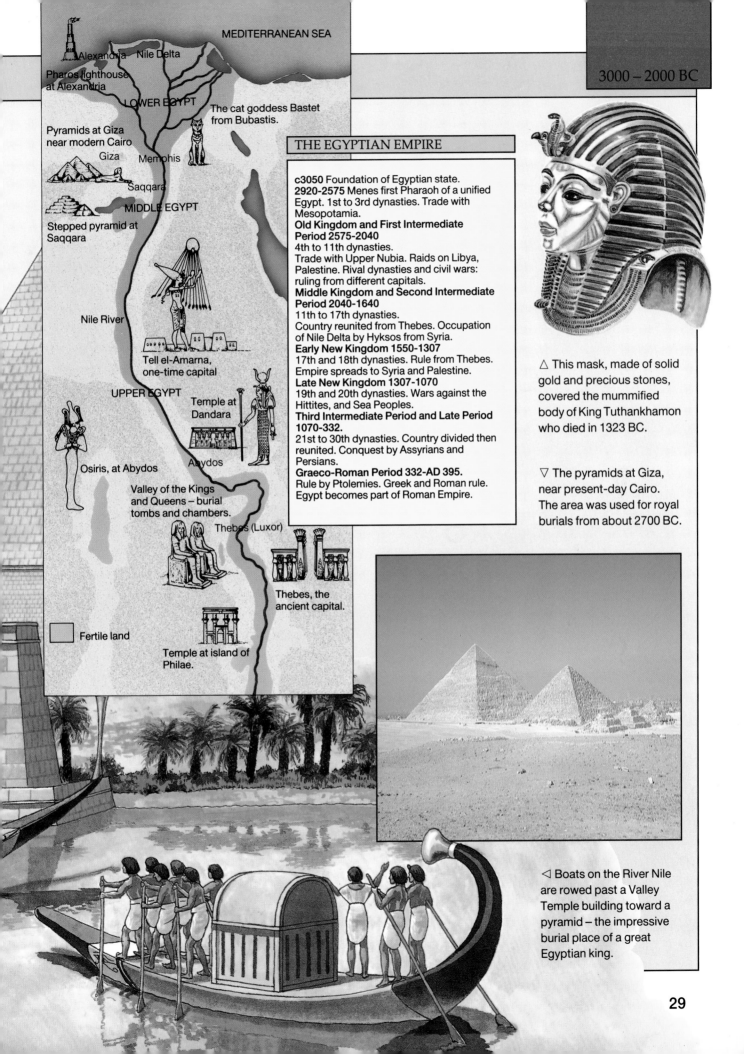

MEDITERRANEAN SEA

Alexandria Nile Delta

Pharos lighthouse
at Alexandria

LOWER EGYPT

The cat goddess Bastet
from Bubastis.

Pyramids at Giza
near modern Cairo

Giza

Memphis

Saqqara

MIDDLE EGYPT

Stepped pyramid at
Saqqara

Nile River

Tell el-Amarna,
one-time capital

UPPER EGYPT

Temple at
Dandara

Osiris, at Abydos

Abydos

Valley of the Kings
and Queens – burial
tombs and chambers.

Thebes (Luxor)

Thebes, the
ancient capital.

Fertile land

Temple at island of
Philae.

THE EGYPTIAN EMPIRE

c3050 Foundation of Egyptian state.
2920-2575 Menes first Pharaoh of a unified
Egypt. 1st to 3rd dynasties. Trade with
Mesopotamia.
**Old Kingdom and First Intermediate
Period 2575-2040**
4th to 11th dynasties.
Trade with Upper Nubia. Raids on Libya,
Palestine. Rival dynasties and civil wars:
ruling from different capitals.
**Middle Kingdom and Second Intermediate
Period 2040-1640**
11th to 17th dynasties.
Country reunited from Thebes. Occupation
of Nile Delta by Hyksos from Syria.
Early New Kingdom 1550-1307
17th and 18th dynasties. Rule from Thebes.
Empire spreads to Syria and Palestine.
Late New Kingdom 1307-1070
19th and 20th dynasties. Wars against the
Hittites, and Sea Peoples.
**Third Intermediate Period and Late Period
1070-332.**
21st to 30th dynasties. Country divided then
reunited. Conquest by Assyrians and
Persians.
Graeco-Roman Period 332-AD 395.
Rule by Ptolemies. Greek and Roman rule.
Egypt becomes part of Roman Empire.

△ This mask, made of solid
gold and precious stones,
covered the mummified
body of King Tuthankhamon
who died in 1323 BC.

▽ The pyramids at Giza,
near present-day Cairo.
The area was used for royal
burials from about 2700 BC.

◁ Boats on the River Nile
are rowed past a Valley
Temple building toward a
pyramid – the impressive
burial place of a great
Egyptian king.

29

EMPIRE BUILDING

The civilized peoples of the Near East who had developed strong and wealthy states now set about extending their influence and building empires.

Wealthy states

Organized farming on a large scale created wealth for these early civilizations. Often there was more food than was immediately needed by the people living there. This surplus food was used to support a growing population and could be traded beyond the territories of a civilization. Surplus food meant that not everyone had to be a farmer. The very first civilizations had had their specialists, such as craftspeople and artists. In this period much larger numbers of people, including workers and soldiers, could be supported by the extra food.

The way in which food was produced, from crops and animals, was highly organized. In some places, such as Mesopotamia and Egypt, the annual floods of the rivers which washed natural fertilizers on to the fields were controlled by canals and irrigation channels. In other areas, such as Greece and South America, terraces on hillsides were created as fields for crops. At the same time, in parts of Europe forests were cut down to make way for fields.

Warfare

Perhaps the most important development during this period was organized warfare between states wealthy enough to support an army. The evidence for warfare comes from two main sources. First, towns in all the important states at this time were heavily defended with walls, gates and towers. If possible, the site chosen for a town was already protected by its natural position. Mycenae (see page 33), on top of a hill, and Wasserburg (see page 34), on an island, are good examples of this. Both these places were also given huge added defences to stave off armies – Wasserburg of wood, Mycenae of enormous blocks of stone.

Second, we now begin to see a whole

▽ It was in this period that the established civilizations increased their territory and built their empires – creating impressive capital cities with royal palaces.

While empire-building was concentrated around the Mediterranean and Near East, cilivizations in China and South America were also developing rapidly.

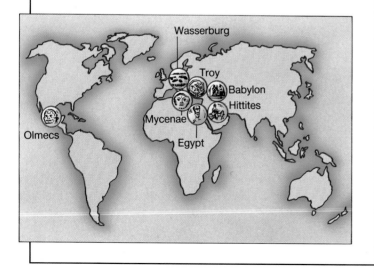

2000-1500 BC

2040 Middle Kingdom in Egypt, pyramids and rock-cut tombs.
2000 Palaces and cities of Minoan civilization on Crete.
2000 Hittites invade Anatolia.
2000 Hsia dynasty in China, beginnings of metalworking.
2000 Maize cultivation and pottery-making in South America. Settlements in Mesoamerica.
1900 Decline of Indus Valley civilization.
1800 Assyria established as an empire, invasion of northern Babylonia.
1792 King Hammurapi begins reign at Babylon.
1600 Shang dynasty in China begins.
1500 Mycenaean civilization established.

1500 – 1000 BC

1500 Aryan peoples invade northern India.
1450 Eruption on Thera. Minoan civilization destroyed.
1323 King Tuthankhamon of Egypt buried.
1200 First civilizations in Mesoamerica. Rise of the Olmecs.
1200 Mycenaeans under threat. Invasion of Sea Peoples. Collapse of Hittite Empire.
1100 Phoenicia powerful in the Mediterranean.
1000 Phoenician alphabet introduced.
1000 Large settlements in the Andes.
1000 Kingdom of Israel under King David.

variety of weapons and armor. Some peoples, like the Hittites (see page 32), began to use chariots in battle. Others, such as the Babylonians and Assyrians, developed special weapons and machines with which to besiege enemy cities. Horses were used in warfare by many peoples. Warships, as well as trading vessels, were built by the Mycenaeans. They fought from their ships and used them to transport armies.

▶ NEW KINGDOM EGYPT

From 1640 BC Egypt was ruled by a foreign dynasty called the Hyksos – people who had traveled to northern Egypt from Palestine. In 1550 BC (from when Egypt was known as the New Kingdom) the king Ahmose drove out the Hyksos and re-established control over all Egypt. With a large professional army New Kingdom Egypt became very powerful, building an empire in Palestine and Syria as well as taking complete control over Nubia on the southern stretches of the Nile. Egyptian influence is shown by the style of furniture and wall and pillar decoration of this wealthy Nubian's house of about 1410 BC.

A Nubian's house

▶ BABYLON

Babylonian clay tablet

When the Amorites invaded Mesopotamia they founded a new capital to replace Ur. It was called Babylon. Under the great king Hammurapi (shown here), Babylon controlled a large empire by conquering all the neighbouring kingdoms. It was King Hammurapi who was the true founder of Babylonian civilization. Hammurapi shifted power to the capital, Babylon, and to the northern part of the Babylonian kingdom. But when Hammurapi died in 1750 BC the Babylonian Empire he created gradually broke up.

Hammurapi was well known for setting out nearly 300 laws for his people. The inset shows part of a clay tablet on which laws were written. Here is a translation of one of Hammurapi's laws:

If a citizen has put out a citizen's eye, they shall put out his eye. If a citizen has broken a citizen's bone, they shall break his bone.

This idea of justice can also be seen in the Old Testament of the Bible – 'an eye for an eye, a tooth for a tooth'.

31

This the Mycenaeans did when they attacked the city of Troy in Turkey in the legendary war of about 1250 BC (see page 35).

More territory and larger cities

Some states, such as Egypt, took over more territory during this period or began to enlarge their cities. All organized states at this time were putting up more and bigger buildings in their cities. Each state had royal palaces, for example at Bogazkoy. These palaces became more and more elaborate as the kings and princes used the wealth of the state to emphasize their own importance.

Religion too was much more organized in this period and generally under state control. More temples and shrines were built in the towns and cities. In about 1300 BC Bogazkoy had five enormous temples. The Olmecs of South America (see page 35) built a number of huge religious ceremonial centers in the small area they controlled.

The first empires

When individual states become wealthier and stronger they often try to increase their territory by conquering other lands and establishing an empire. It was during this period that empires were developing in three main areas – the Near East, Egypt and the eastern Mediterranean.

Egypt was very well protected by natural barriers. The marshy delta where the River Nile flowed into the Mediterranean, the rapids on the rivers in the far south, the mountains and the deserts, all made it difficult to invade.

But in the Near East, where the first civilizations had developed, states had few natural defences and could easily be attacked. For example, in about 2000 BC the power of Ur (see page 22) faded when a nomadic people, the Amorites, invaded this area and established the capital of Babylon.

⊙ BOGAZKOY – HITTITE CAPITAL

Bogazkoy, now in Turkey, was once the capital city of the Hittites and called Hattushash. There was originally a fortress here which used the natural defences offered by its position on the headland. In about 1650 BC it became the capital of the Hittite Empire. Double walls surrounded a huge area of the city. The upper part of Bogazkoy was itself defended with a stone wall. Inside was a great temple and palace as well as a strongly fortified citadel.

Hittite charioteer outside the capital city's walls

Mycenaean death mask

MYCENAE

2000 Mycenaean people first appear in Greece. They either migrated from central Europe to Greece or their culture developed from people already there.
1600 Small Mycenaean kingdoms develop. People buried in shaft graves.
1500 Mycenaean kingdoms now at their most powerful, on both mainland Greece and neighbouring islands. Beehive-shaped tombs (called *tholoi*) now appear.
1450 Volcanic eruption on island of Thera. Minoan civilization on Crete destroyed. Mycenaeans occupy and govern Crete.
1250 Mycenaean forces attack city of Troy.
1200 Mycenaean kingdoms under threat. Strong city walls and Lion Gate built at Mycenae.
1150 Cities gradually abandoned. Mycenae destroyed. End of Mycenaean civilization.
1100 Mainland Greeks begin to emigrate to the coasts of Asia Minor (now Turkey).

▷ ▽ A beaten gold funeral mask of one of the Mycenaean kings (right), found in the grave circle just inside the city walls. (Below) The city of Mycenae, capital of the empire. In the center is the royal palace and courtyard.

△ Sparta
● Athens
◆ Mycenae
◇ Pylos
▲ Troy

▲ ▶ MYCENAE

Mycenae was the capital of an empire in southern Greece. The empire consisted of a number of small kingdoms each with its own fortified settlement, like Mycenae itself, pictured above. It was a rich and powerful empire, which traded as far east as Egypt and the coast of Lebanon, and as far west as Italy and Sardinia. In about 1550 BC Mycenae took control of the eastern Mediterranean, which had earlier been ruled by the Minoans of Crete (see page 24). Mycenae itself was a well-defended hilltop town, called an acropolis. Its walls were made of massive blocks of stone. The entrance was topped by two massive lions carved in stone – the Lion Gate. There were tombs for the kings and nobles both inside and outside the city walls. The earliest tombs were shafts sunk more than 40 feet into the ground. Later the Mycenaean Greeks built huge elaborate beehive-shaped tombs such as the one shown on the right.

Beehive-shaped tomb

Later the region of Ur and Babylon was invaded and occupied by the victorious Assyrian armies (see page 39).

It was not only in the Near East and the Mediterranean that new civilizations and empires were being created. Kings of the Shang dynasty, the first civilization in China (see pages 36-7), also controlled large territories. The first real civilization in South

▼ THE WASSERBURG

From about 2000 BC more and more settlements in northern Europe were being fortified. Communities increasingly attacked each other to fight for control of territories. In southern Germany, in the Federsee lake, is an island known as the Wasserburg. The island was first occupied by about 40 wooden houses around 1200 BC. This settlement of farmers was strongly defended by its wooden palisade walls and gates made from over 150,000 timber posts.

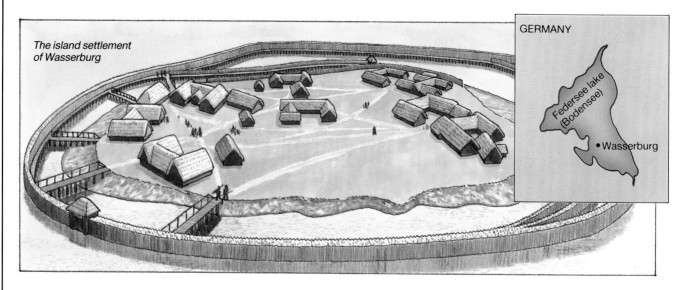

The island settlement of Wasserburg

GERMANY

Federsee lake (Bodensee)

• Wasserburg

America, that of the Olmecs, was established around 1200 BC. The Olmecs were not peaceful people but neither did they build a great empire for themselves.

The written record
Although writing had been invented some time before (see page 25), it is from this period onwards that archaeologists and historians are able to use a large number of records. We know, for example, how big an area of Palestine owed loyalty to the powerful Egyptians, because of letters recorded on clay tablets. Clay tablets from Mycenae give us information about a whole range of different jobs – from coastguards to priests. For some empires we can read the names both of kings and of others less important.

MEDITERRANEAN
2000 Palaces and harbor cities of Minoan civilization on Crete. **1900** Hieroglyphic writing used in Crete. **1650** Writing known as Linear A used in Crete. **1500** Mycenaean civilization established. **1450** Eruption on Thera, end of Minoan civilization. Mycenaeans now most important power in Greece and the islands. **1400** Writing called Linear B used in Greece. **1200** Mycenaeans build defensive settlements. Sea Peoples overwhelm parts of Mediterranean and Near East. Phoenician cities take over trade in eastern Mediterranean. **1100** Phoenicia establishes colonies. **1000** Phoenician alphabet introduced.

EGYPT
2040 Middle Kingdom in Egypt. Country reunited and ruled from Thebes. Trade with Syria and Palestine. **1652** War between Egypt and the Hyksos peoples from Asia, who take over much of country. **1550** The Hyksos driven out of Egypt. New Kingdom of Egypt established. **1469** Egyptian King Tuthmosis III extends territory by military power. **1367** New king adopts the name Akhenaten and establishes new captital at Amarna. **1323** King Tuthankhamon of Egypt buried. **1218** and **1182** Invasion of Egypt by the Sea Peoples. **1070** New Kingdom of Egypt comes to an end.

The walled city of Troy

◀ THE CITY OF TROY

The city of Troy, now called Hissarlik in Turkey, was very well known to the ancient Greeks, as it is to us today, because of an epic poem by Homer. Homer's poem, the *Iliad*, was probably composed about 750 BC. It records a great war between the Greeks, led by the Mycenaean king Agamemnon, and the Trojans. The *Iliad* tells how, after a long siege, the Trojans were tricked into opening the gates of their city to the enemy. They found a wooden horse outside which they believed to be a gift from the gods but it turned out to be full of Greek soldiers from Mycenae. If such a war did take place it was probably about 1250 BC, when the Mycenaeans were establishing their territory in the eastern Mediterranean.

▼ THE OLMECS

The Olmecs lived on a thin strip of land between the Gulf of Mexico and the Pacific Ocean. Their civilization began around 1200 BC when they built ceremonial centers for their religion. The Olmecs created stone monuments and earth mounds in these ceremonial centers. Olmec sculptors made colossal carvings, like this one of a head from San Lorenzo. The Olmecs traded with other peoples from as far away as central Mexico and Costa Rica. Their civilization seems to have come to an end around 400 BC.

NEAR EAST, ASIA

2000 Canaanites invade the empire founded by Sargon I of Akkad. Hittites move into Anatolia.
1900 Decline of cities of the Indus Valley civilization in India.
1800 Assyrians invade northern Babylonia. Fall of the Third Dynasty at Ur. Assyria established as an empire.
1792-1750 Hammurapi reigns from Babylon.
1500 Aryan peoples invade northern India.
1250 Israelite tribes move from Egypt and establish League of 12 Tribes in Israel.
1200 Hittite Empire collapses.
1000 Kingdom of Israel under King David.

PACIFIC

2205-1766 Hsia dynasty in China begins – first emperor Yu. Walled settlements and metalworking introduced.
1600 Shang dynasty in China begins. Capital at Zhengzhou.
1500 The Lapita people of Polynesia spread to Samoa and Tonga. Rice farming in Korea.
1400 Shang dynasty capital moves to Anyang. First Chinese written inscriptions.
1027 Chou Hsin, last Shang king overthrown.
1027-256 Chou dynasty in China.
1000 Peoples reach almost every island in Polynesia. Working in bronze reaches Korea from Manchuria. Long-distance trade by peoples in Australia.

AMERICAS

2300 Settlements in Mesoamerica. Earliest pottery in Mesoamerica.
2000 Earliest pottery made in Andes region of South America. Maize cultivated on a large scale. Inuits (Eskimos) reach northern part of Greenland.
1500 First metalworking in Peru. Hunting peoples in North America build villages for seasonal hunts. Called the Archaic Period.
1200 First civilizations in Mesoamerica based on cities. Beginning of the Olmec civilization.
1000 People of the eastern woodlands in North America build mounds over rich burials. Large settlements built in the Andes region.

THE SHANG DYNASTY

The first civilization to develop in China was under the Shang dynasty, which began around 1600 BC. The Shang kings ruled northern China until the warlike Chou people conquered the land in 1027 BC. A lot of information is known about the Shang from recently excavated burials of kings at Anyang.

Capitals of the Shang dynasty

The first capital, Zhengzhou, was a large enclosure protected by walls of earth. The palace of the king was built on a raised platform. Outside the walls were houses, workshops, pottery kilns and metal foundries. Later, in the 13th century BC, the Shang dynasty moved the capital from Zhengzhou to Anyang.

The Shang kings

In Shang society the king claimed that he was descended from the supreme god, called Shang Ti, who founded the world. The king was in complete control of the Shang world. He commanded the army, collected taxes from the people and was in

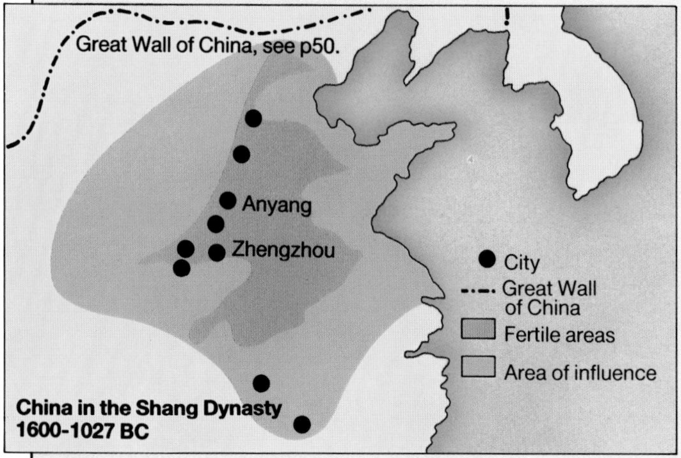

Great Wall of China, see p50.

Anyang

Zhengzhou

● City
–·–· Great Wall of China
Fertile areas
Area of influence

China in the Shang Dynasty 1600-1027 BC

◁ There were many villages and towns, apart from the capital, in the large Shang territory.

▽ Burials of Shang kings and nobles showed what power they had over the people, who were little more than slaves. At the entrance to the burial pit animals and people were sacrificed and laid out.

Shang Capital of Anyang

CHINA'S EARLY DYNASTIES

3000 Society in China evolving. Stone tools still used.
2205-1766 Hsia dynasty. Yu is China's first emperor. Walled settlements and the introduction of metalworking.
1600 Beginning of the Shang dynasty. First capital at Zhengzhou. Bronze metalworking flourishes.
1400 Capital moved from Zhengzhou to Anyang on the Huan River. Surviving records tell of 12 kings ruling here for 273 years. Many tombs of royal families and nobles excavated, including burials of whole chariots with horses and drivers. First written inscriptions in China at this time.
1027 Last Shang king, Chou Hsin, overthrown. The Shang dynasty comes to an end. Chou dynasty controls the western part of the country. Chou dynasty divided into Western and Eastern dynasties. Cast iron invented in this period.
551-479 Period of Confucius, famous Chinese philosopher.
770 Capital of Chou dynasty moves to Luoyang. Start of Eastern Chou dynasty.
481-221 Central authority breaks down as nobles fight for control of their own lands from fortified cities. Called the period of the Warring States.
221 Ch'in Shi-huang-ti unites country and founds new dynasty, calling himself 'First Emperor'. He establishes a new system of government.
214 Emperor Ch'in begins Great Wall of China.
On his death, life-size models of all the workers who built his great tomb are buried with him.
207 Han dynasty founded.

charge of the great irrigation schemes. These schemes made it possible for farmers to grow crops such as rice, millet and wheat. Farmers also kept animals including sheep, cattle, horses, goats, pigs and dogs.

When a Shang king, or his queen, died, an elaborate burial pit was constructed. Together with the dead ruler, other humans and animals were buried alive. The tomb of one Shang queen buried at Anyang contained 16 human victims and 6 dogs. These tombs also held large numbers of objects, including bronze vessels, jade ornaments and cowrie shells from the Pacific Ocean. Cowrie shells were used as a form of money in Shang China.

△ This ritual vessel held fragrant wine offered to the ancestors; from the tomb of a Shang king.

GREAT CIVILIZATIONS

A Chavin temple

Peoples who lived around, and especially on the coasts of, the Mediterranean Sea became very important from about 1000 BC. There was now much more contact between peoples, often brought about by trade. The most frequent traders, the Phoenicians (see page 41), became very rich by exporting what grew, or could be made, in their own country and exchanging this with goods elsewhere. The Phoenicians carried other people's goods as well as their own. They also invented their own alphabet, which was later used by the Greeks and then the Romans and spread to the rest of Europe.

Wealthy peoples

Wealth could be taken from defeated enemies or extracted as taxes, but wealthy

▽ In the lands that bordered the Mediterranean Sea and in the Fertile Crescent a number of major civilizations arose. Some of them also looked for new lands and founded colonies. In the Americas and in China, new ways of life were also being established.

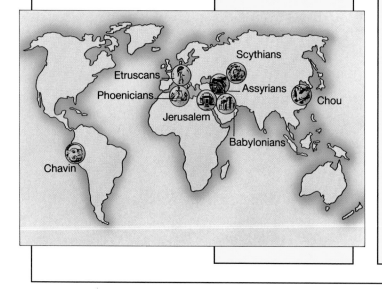

1000 – 900 BC
1000 Woodland cultures develop in North America.
1000 Phoenician trading in Mediterranean. Phoenician alphabet developed.
1000 Kingdom of Israel founded with capital in Jerusalem.
1000 Etruscans arrive in Italy.
900 New Assyrian Empire
900 Chavin civilization begins in South America.

900 – 500 BC
900 City-state of Sparta established.
880 Assyrian capital moved to Nimrud.
850 First settlement on the site of Rome.
814 Phoenician city of Carthage founded.
800 Greeks first use Phoenician writing.
800 City-states established along the Ganges River, India.
800 Maize cultivated along River Amazon, South America.
776 First Olympic Games.
770 Eastern Chou dynasty, China.
753 Traditional date for the foundation of Rome.
750 Greek colonies in Mediterranean.
700 Scythians move into eastern Europe from Asia.
689 Assyrians take Babylon.
671 Assyrians conquer Egypt.
612 Assyrian Empire falls.
600 Phoenicians sail around Africa.
550 Sparta most powerful city-state in Greece.
508 Democratic government in Athens.

◉ THE CHAVIN CIVILIZATION

The people of the Andes Mountains in Peru, South America, were farmers. They grew a variety of crops such as potatoes, squash, chilli peppers, beans and maize. They fished and hunted and bred guinea-pigs and ducks for extra food. The people of the Chavin civilization built huge temples. Their name was given to them by archaeologists who excavated one of their sites at Chavin de Huantar. They also produced frightening carvings of animals with human features. In one temple was found the carving of a god 15 feet high which had a snarling mouth with fangs and had snakes in its hair.

civilizations usually had their own major source of income. At this time Athens was the most powerful city-state in Greece because of the silver-mines at Laureion near the city. Precious metals were also a source of wealth for other peoples, such as the Scythians (see page 42). While the Greeks were searching for new lands where they could set up colonies, the Etruscans (see page 43) were moving into northern Italy to become rich farmers and fine metalworkers and pottery manufacturers.

People with their own identity
An important development in this period was that of self-government. Whereas the Phoenicians invented a new alphabet, the Greeks developed the idea of the city-state.

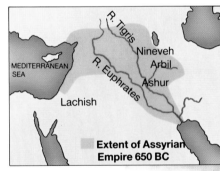

Extent of Assyrian Empire 650 BC

Assyrian forces besiege Lachish

▶ THE ASSYRIANS

Assyrian power began around 2000 BC. It centered on three city states – Nineveh, Ashur and Arbil (see map). From about about 1363 BC the king Ashur-uballit I began to build a great empire. It was an empire founded on military might, as Assyrian armies, under successive kings, increased the territory they controlled. They took over the kingdom of Ur in Babylonia, conquered Egypt and controlled the eastern part of the Mediterranean Sea. The picture shows the siege of Lachish (now in Israel) by King Sennacherib in 701 BC. The Assyrians built a ramp to bring their siege engines close to the walls of Lachish. Sennacherib had friezes carved on the walls of his palace at Nineveh to record the event.

⊙ JERUSALEM UNDER SOLOMON

David became king of Judah in about 1000 BC, and
established his palace at Hebron, east of the Dead Sea. He
defeated the Philistines (Palestinians) in war and captured
Jerusalem, which he made the capital of the kingdom of
Israel. After his death in about 960 BC, his son Solomon
became king. From the Bible we know Solomon was famous
for his wisdom. We also know him from his building projects.
This is his temple to Yahweh (God) in Jerusalem.

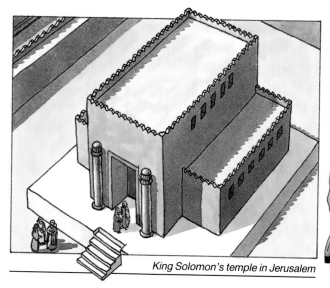

King Solomon's temple in Jerusalem

⊙ THE CHOU DYNASTY IN CHINA

In 1027 BC the Chou state to the north of Anyang, the capital
of the Shang dynasty (see page 36), overthrew the last
Shang king. The kings of the Chou dynasty maintained
control by granting their own relatives and other nobles the
right to rule small areas themselves. Eventually central
authority broke down and the period of Warring States
began in 481 BC. During the Chou dynasty iron was cast
and coins were first used from around 500 BC.

Chou king and nobles

MEDITERRANEAN

1100 Mainland Greeks
settle in Asia Minor.
1000 Etruscans, probably
from West Asia, begin to
arrive in Tuscany, Italy.
1000 David anointed King
of Israel at Hebron.
960-922 Solomon king of
Israel. Great rebuilding
and Temple in Jerusalem.
922 Israel divided after
Solomon's death.
900-800 Establishment of
Etruscan cities.
850 First settlement on
the site of Rome.
814 Carthage established
as new city of
Phoenicians.
c800 Greeks adopt
Phoenician writing.
753 Traditional date for
foundation of Rome.
722 Israel an Assyrian
province.
700 Etruscan writing
develops from Greek.
509 Last Etruscan king,
Tarquin the Proud,
expelled by the Romans.

MESOPOTAMIA

883-859 Under
Ashurnasirpal II Assyrian
armies extend conquered
territory. Cavalry used for
the first time in warfare.
744-727 Tiglath-pileser III
continues Assyrian
conquests.
721-705 Assyrian Empire
expanded under Sargon I.
704-681 Sennacherib
wages war with Babylonia
and sacks it in **689**. He
tries but fails to capture
Jerusalem.
668-627 Ashurbanipal
takes over control of the
Assyrian Empire. Babylon
taken in **648**.
625-539 New Babylonian
Empire established.
604-562 Nebuchadnezzar
II rebuilds and enlarges
Babylon (and builds
Tower of Babel).
587 Jerusalem captured
by Babylonians.
539 Conquest of
Babylonia by Persian
king, Cyrus II.

FAR EAST

1027 Last Shang king,
Chou Hsin, overthrown.
Shang dynasty comes to
an end. Chou dynasty
now controls west of
country.
1000 Lapita peoples
reach Tonga and Samoa
islands of Polynesia.
Bronze-making reaches
Korea from Manchuria.
Rice cultivation
introduced to southern
Japan from China.
770 Capital of Chou
dynasty moves to
Luoyang. Start of Eastern
Chou dynasty.
500 Cast iron first used in
China for agricultural tools
and weapons.
Chinese 'coins' first used
– in fact, miniature bronze
spades and knives with
inscriptions.
500 Wet rice cultivation in
Japan.

AMERICAS

1000 Peoples in eastern
woodlands of North
America build burial and
ceremonial mounds.
Large communities in the
Andes region of South
America.
Dorset hunting people
spread across the Arctic.
900 Chavin civilization in
the Andes.
Oldest known Olmec
center of San Lorenzo
destroyed in
Mesoamerica. La Venta
becomes main centre.
800 Zapotec people in
Mesoamerica produce the
first writing in the
Americas.
Maize cultivation on a
large scale in the Andes
region.
500 Ipiutak villages of up
to 700 houses on coast of
Alaska.

⦿ THE PHOENICIANS

Phoenicia was the name given by the Greeks to the coastal lands of what is now mostly Lebanon and Israel. The Phoenicians themselves seem to have been a mixture of Canaanites and peoples from other countries such as Greece and Cyprus. They built important coastal towns with harbors – Tyre, Sidon and Byblos. From there they became the most important and powerful traders across the Mediterranean Sea, using their forests to build ships. They also exported timber as well as finely-made glass vases and beads and a purple dye made from a shellfish called murex. Besides trading, the Phoenicians established their own new language and colonies, in particular Carthage on the North African coast (see the map below). Known as Carthaginians, they later clashed with the Romans (see pages 52-3).

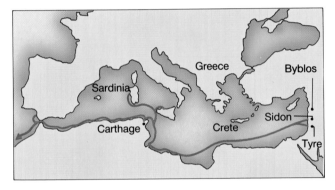

▽ Small Phoenician merchant boats like this carried goods across the Mediterranean.

To feel important and strong, people living in a city, Athens, Corinth, Argos or Sparta for example, also controlled the territory around. They governed themselves but were still all Greeks, sometimes joining together against a common enemy, such as the Persians (see page 47). But Sparta and Athens developed quite differently from each other and even went to war (see page 44). Athens evolved the democratic form of government (see page 45), while Sparta was governed by a small ruling class made up of the military.

Extraordinary buildings

From the very first civilizations, powerful rulers had built grand structures for reasons of ceremony, religion, government or defence. Now new types of structures began to emerge, with new artists employed to make them attractive. For example, King Nebuchadnezzar (see page 43) built the famous Hanging Gardens for his wife in his royal capital Babylon.

Just as extraordinary was the rebuilding of the central religious area of Athens. The Acropolis with its temples had been destroyed by the Persians (see time chart, page 44) but new building work started and in 447 BC the most important temple was begun. This was the Parthenon, the temple to the city's special goddess, Athena, who gave the city her name. A statue to her, 43 feet tall, by the sculptor Pheidias, once stood inside the huge temple (see page 45).

THE PHOENICIANS

c1200 Decline of power of Cretan and Mycenaean peoples. Phoenician cities take over trade in eastern Mediterranean.
c1100 Rise in power of independent Phoenician cities of Tyre, Byblos, Beirut, Sidon and Aradus.
1000 Phoenician writing developed. Azarbaal earliest recorded Phoenican king.
969-936 King Hiram I reigning in Tyre. Trade developed in Mediterranean and in the Red Sea. Trade treaties with King Solomon.
900-600 Phoenician colonies established overseas.
701 Phoenicia conquered by Assyrian king Sennacherib.
666 City of Tyre taken by Assyrians.

Colonies and conquests

Often, when a people or a strong ruler establishes an identity, they want to spread their way of life or take over other people's lands. Greeks, Phoenicians and Etruscans were all seeking new lands and so they set up colonies. The Assyrians (see page 39) had a different approach. They used their well-equipped, large armies to conquer new lands. At the height of their power, by 626 BC, they controlled a huge area east from the Persian Gulf almost to the Black Sea and west to the mouth of the River Nile.

Writing, records and propaganda

For some civilizations at this time, detailed written records still exist which help us find out what life must have been like. For example, Greek history was well recorded by historians of the time and through inscriptions and sculpture.

The Assyrian kings also had sculpture and inscriptions made to record their history. It is from sculpture, for example, that we know how King Sennacherib besieged Lachish in 701 BC. The same king had an inscription cut to record his siege of Jerusalem. Part of it reads,

Hezekiah, the Judaean, I shut up in Jerusalem like a bird in a cage. I surrounded him with watchposts and made it impossible for anyone to go in or out of his city.

We also have another important written source for this period – the Bible. It has often been possible to check the findings of archaeologists against the Bible.

Other parts of the world

During this period, in South America we see the beginnings of the Chavin civilization in Peru (see page 38). Also, the Zapotec people in Mesoamerica produced the continent's first evidence of writing. Meanwhile in China powerful nobles eventually caused the downfall of central government (see page 40), leading to the period of Warring States.

⊽ ▶ THE SCYTHIANS

The Scythians were nomadic peoples who probably came originally from central Asia but who migrated south to the shores of the Black Sea and the Caspian Sea. They moved about, grazing herds of cattle and hunting, but some did make permanent settlements in the good farming land of their southern territory. The nomadic Scythians travelled across country in felt-covered wagons. Scythian nobles were wealthy and buried gold objects in graves. Some of these tombs have been preserved in frozen ground.

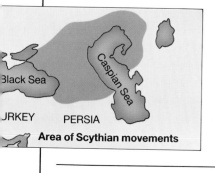

Area of Scythian movements

Black Sea

Caspian Sea

URKEY   PERSIA

▷ Some of the tombs of rich Scythians in the Pazyryk Valley of southern Siberia had their contents preserved by continuous ice since the 5th century BC. This detail of an amphora shows Scythians training horses.

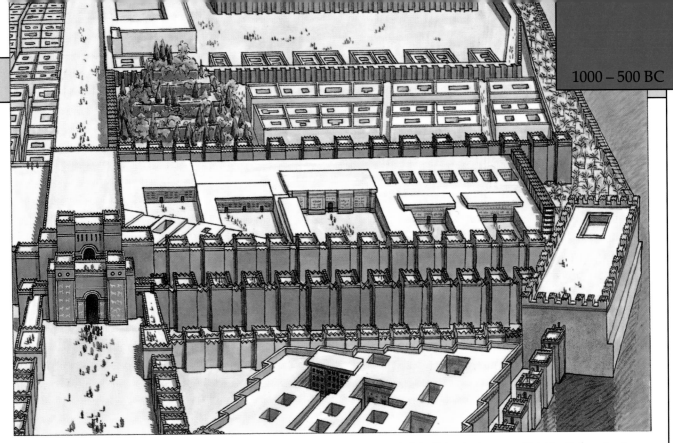

Babylon, rebuilt by Nebuchadnezzar, with Ishtar Gate and walls

⊛ NEBUCHADNEZZAR'S BABYLON

The independent kingdom of Babylonia had been fought over and occupied by several peoples, including the Assyrians. Sometimes the Babylonians managed to maintain peace with their neighbours, sometimes they had to fight. In 605 BC a commander who became the most famous of all Babylonian kings, Nebuchadnezzar II, had to beat off the Egyptians. Nebuchadnezzar is especially known for the rebuilding of the capital city, Babylon. The main entrance to the defended city was through the Ishtar Gate, covered with brightly-colored tiles. The gate was named

after the Mesopotamian goddess of war, whose sacred beasts (lions, bulls and dragons) decorated its walls. From this gate a ceremonial path led past the palace of the king to the huge Temple of Marduk, the god of Babylon. This great ziggurat, similar to the one in Ur (see page 23), dominated the city. But Babylon was best known for its Hanging Gardens, – one of the Seven Wonders of the Ancient World. The beautiful terraced gardens were said to have been built to remind Nebuchadnezzar's wife, Amitiya, daughter of the king of the Medes, of her mountainous homeland.

⊛ THE ETRUSCANS

Etruria, the area to the north of Rome in Italy, was the home of the Etruscans from about 900 BC. Their language has been lost, but we still know a lot about them from their remains and because many of the later Roman buildings and customs were copied from the Etruscans. Etruscan cities were each independent with a separate government though the inhabitants thought of themselves first and foremost as Etruscans. They were very rich people, most of them farmers who traded with the Greeks. Etruscan nobles had elaborate underground tombs prepared for when they died. The tombs, like this one at Cerveteri, were built like houses and then decorated and filled with furniture and treasures. Great mounds of earth on the surface marked the locations of the underground tombs.

Underground tomb at Cerveteri

THE GREEK EMPIRE

The Greek Empire was at first a world divided into a large number of city-states. By modern standards there were not many people living in each city-state but they constantly quarrelled and fought each other. Each wanted more power and more territory. In particular there were two very powerful city-states – Athens and Sparta – who eventually engaged each other in a conflict known as the Peloponnesian War.

The city of Athens

Athens had been a Mycenaean city (see page 33). Its kings had lived on a defended hill in the city center called the Acropolis, the 'high city'. This became the place of the temples to the Greek gods and goddesses but was destroyed by the invading Persians in 480 BC. New building started in 447 BC

on the most famous temple of all, the Parthenon, dedicated to the goddess Athena, whom the Greeks believed sprang from the head of Zeus, the king of the gods.

Athens, and some other Greek city-states, had a special form of government which they called *demokratia* – democracy. All

---

GREEK EMPIRE

1500 Mycenaean period. Kingdoms on mainland Greece including Mycenae and Pylos.
1150 Mycenae destroyed.
1000 Mainland Greeks begin to emigrate to Asia Minor.
850-750 Homer, writer of epic poems, may have lived during this time.
776 First Olympic Games held at Olympia.
750 Greek colonies founded in Sicily and southern Italy.
550 Sparta the most powerful state in southern Greece.
508 Democratic government in Athens.
490 Persians invade Athens but are defeated at Marathon.
480-479 Persians invade Greece, sack Athens and destroy the Acropolis. Alliance formed against them led by Athens. Athenian Empire begins.
480 Persian fleet defeated at Battle of Salamis.
479 Greeks defeat Persian army at Battle of Plataea.
447 Building of the Parthenon begins.
431-404 Peloponnesian War between Athens and Sparta, won by Sparta.
358 Macedonia (northern Greece) unified under Philip II.
334 Alexander the Great's campaign against the Persians.
333 Alexander defeats the Persian army at the Battle of Issos.

Athenian citizens (which excluded women and slaves) came together about every nine days on the hill overlooking the Agora, the great public square in the city. Citizens argued, made speeches and debated how to run their city-state. Five or six thousand people would usually attend.

Issos

Sicily

Asia Minor

Greece

Italy

Plataea

Athens

Olympia   Salamis

Sparta

MEDITERRANEAN SEA

The Greek Empire

◁ The Greeks established colonies of city-states in southern Italy and Sicily, in North Africa and on the coasts of Asia Minor.

△ ▽ In 500 BC Athens had a population of 250,000. Houses (above) usually had courtyards. (Below) The Parthenon today.

◁ The Agora, below the Acropolis, was the place for business, ceremonies and government buildings. Here, in the shady colonnades, Athenians discussed politics and philosophy.

TRADE AND WARFARE

Persian forces land at Marathon

Civilizations with strong identities have wanted to spread their ideas and influence into other peoples' lands. Greek civilization under Alexander the Great and, later the Romans were ambitious in this way. As world powers emerged, so they engaged in world wars – the Greeks against the Persians, and the Romans against the Celtic peoples.

Trade and cultural connections

Contact between peoples also increased through trade and culture as life became more complex and people developed more sophisticated tastes. Some wanted new materials for building, others admired the crafts of far-off peoples while others simply needed more food than they could produce at home for their increasing populations. There were many routes of communications and trade at this time. The most famous is the Silk Road (see page 51), which connected the Far East with western Europe.

A major breakthrough in cultural contact between peoples came with the development of the arts and literature of individual civilizations. The Ancient Greeks were

◉ THE BATTLE OF MARATHON

The Persians under their king Darius I (see opposite) had crushed Greek revolts in Asia Minor (now Turkey) and in 490 BC sent an army across to mainland Greece. They completely destroyed the town of Eretria, which had helped the Greeks in Asia Minor against the Persians, and now crossed to the eastern coast nearest to the city of Athens. In the Bay of Marathon about 24,000 Persians waited for battle. The Greeks had a force of about 10,000, mainly Athenians with some men from Plataea. When the Persian force finally landed on 12 September 490 BC, the two strong wings of the Greek army enveloped the Persians and killed about 6,400 of them. The Athenians lost only 192 men. A messenger was said to have run the 26 miles to Athens to bring news of the victory.

famous not only for their fine buildings and sculpture but also for their literature. The Romans were great admirers of Greek civilization. In fact several Roman emperors adopted Greek customs – Hadrian for example. Meanwhile, in the Han dynasty of China, which lasted some 200 years, the most beautiful objects were created from precious stones and metals.

⊙ ALEXANDER THE GREAT

In 336 BC Alexander became King of Macedonia, in northern Greece. Between then and his death in 323 he conquered a huge empire and became known as Alexander the Great. In 334 he led a force of 12,000 Macedonians and 12,000 other Greeks across to Asia Minor. The next year, at the Battle of Issos, he defeated the Persian King Darius III. This drawing of Alexander is from a Roman mosaic showing the Battle of Issos.

Alexander the Great

⊙ PERSIAN EMPIRE UNDER DARIUS I

Under King Darius I, who came to the throne in 522 BC, the Persian Empire stretched from what is now the coast of Turkey to the River Indus in present-day Pakistan. It also included Egypt. To control and tax a huge population made up of many different peoples, Darius created 23 *satrapies* (provinces) each with its own governor, administrator and financial controller. He also built roads throughout the empire and Persepolis (shown above) as his ceremonial capital.

500 – 300 BC

509 Etruscan king thrown out in Rome. Roman Republic established.
508 Democratic government established in Athens.
500 Revolt by Greek colonies in Asia against Persian rule.
490 Persian invasion army defeated in Greece.
480 Persian invasion of Greece again repulsed.
400 Olmec civilization in America in decline.
390 Celts sack the city of Rome.
334 Alexander the Great begins campaigns against the Persian Empire.
330 Alexander takes the ceremonial Persian capital, Persepolis.

300 BC – AD 1

321 Chandragupta becomes King of Magadha and establishes Mauryan Empire.
300 Early Mayan period in America begins.
270 Asoka becomes Mauryan Emperor.
264 First war between Carthaginians and Romans.
221 China united by first emperor Ch'in Shi-huang-ti.
146 Carthage destroyed by the Romans.
59 Romans invade Gaul.
55 First Roman invasion of Britain.
30 Egypt becomes a Roman province.
27 First Roman Emperor. End of Republic.

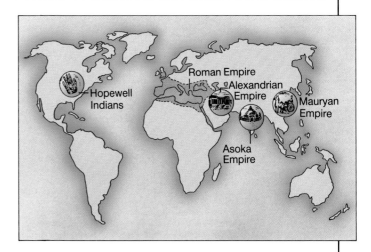

△ After defeating the Persians, Alexander pushed east, conquering many peoples and building towns which were centers of Greek life and culture.

MOUND BUILDERS OF AMERICA

While empires clashed in Europe, in the north-eastern woodlands of North America groups of farmers lived along the tributaries of the Mississippi and Ohio rivers much as they had done for centuries. The people, whom we call the Adena, were prosperous farmers growing enough food to support the large workforces who built great burial mounds and earthworks. This Great Serpent Mound in Ohio is 712 feet long. From about 300 BC the Hopewell people, who were farmers and traders, also built great earthworks, in particular mounds for their dead. They were buried with a variety of rich objects, such as the copper bird shown on the right.

△ Falcon from a Hopewell burial mound in Ohio. It is made of a sheet of copper with feathers and decoration embossed on it.

EUROPE

509 Etruscan king thrown out in Rome. Republic established.
480 Carthaginians defeated by the Greek cities on Sicily.
400 Celts migrate into northern Italy.
390 Celts sack the city of Rome.
380 New defences built around city of Rome.
300 Celtic states formed in Europe. Contact with Greece. First Celtic coins.
298-290 Romans at war with Etruscans, Samnites and Celts.
264 First Roman War against the Carthaginians.
250 All Italy controlled by the Romans.
218-201 Second Roman War with Carthage.
146 Rome finally destroys Carthage, occupies Greece.
100 Celts develop defended settlements – *oppida*.
59-49 Celtic states in Gaul conquered by Romans.
27 First Roman Emperor.

MEDITERRANEAN

508 Democratic government in Athens.
490 Greek revolt against Persian Empire. Persians defeated at Battle of Marathon.
480-479 Persians invade Greece but are defeated. Athenian Empire begins.
447 Parthenon temple in Athens begun.
431-404 War between Athens and Sparta, won by Sparta.
404-371 Spartan Empire.
338 Philip of Macedon conquers Greece.
336 Philip's son, Alexander, succeeds him.
334 Alexander (the Great) invades Persian Empire in Asia.
331 City of Alexandria in Egypt founded by Alexander.
323 Alexander dies.
c200 Alexandria as the centre of Greek science and learning.
146 Greece made into Roman provinces.
30 Egypt made into a Roman province.

ASIA

522 Darius I ruler of the Persian Empire.
500 Revolt by Ionian Greeks against Persia.
492 Persians occupy northern Greece.
486 Xerxes succeeds his father Darius as the Persian ruler.
485-482 Xerxes crushes revolts in Egypt and Babylon.
480 Xerxes attempts to conquer Greece but is defeated.
479 Persian fleet defeated by Greeks at Salamis.
465 Xerxes assassinated.
405 Artaxerxes II the new Persian ruler.
401 Failed revolt by Cyrus the Younger against his brother Artaxerxes.
334 Alexander the Great begins campaigns against Persian Empire. Persians defeated at Battle of Granikos.
333 Second Persian defeat at Battle of Issos.
330 The Persian capital, Persepolis, taken by Alexander.

INDIA, CHINA

493 Ajatashatru, King of Magadha in India.
481-221 Period of the Warring States in China.
479 Confucius, Chinese philosopher, dies.
327-325 Alexander the Great campaigns in India.
321 Chandragupta takes the throne of the kingdom of Magadha, establishes the Mauryan Empire.
304 Seleukos (Alexander's successor in Persia) gives up his Indian territories to Chandragupta.
297 Chandragupta dies.
270-232 Reign of Asoka, Mauryan Empire at its greatest.
221 China united after the period of the Warring States by Emperor Ch'in Shi-huang-ti.
214 Great Wall of China begun.
207-AD9 Han dynasty in China.
185 Mauryan Empire of India in decline.
100 North Vietnam ruled as a Chinese province.

Asia and the Mediterranean

This was the period when Greece emerged as a powerful nation, extending its influence beyond its mainland boundaries. The colonies that were set up in southern Italy, southern Gaul and Asia carried Greek civilization to new peoples. They then followed the Greeks' way of life, their democratic form of government, their architecture, art and literature. But Greece came into conflict with Persia over Asia.

Around 500 BC the Persian Empire was the largest the world had ever seen. By comparison Greece and its islands were tiny. The two civilizations clashed over their borders on the coast of what is now Turkey. Persia tried to add Greece to its empire and failed. The Greeks were fewer in number but they, unlike the Persians, were not just paid soldiers but a people fighting for their own lands. Persia would have remained a threat to Greece if Alexander the Great had not then taken the initiative and invaded the Persian Empire. From his small kingdom of Macedonia in northern Greece, Alexander eventually replaced the huge Persian Empire with his own Greek Empire.

After the Greeks

After Alexander's death his great empire did not hold together. One of Alexander's generals, Seleukos, took control of the Persian area of the Greek Empire. But within this region a new people, the Parthians, gradually gained more territory and established their own empire. In Egypt the Ptolemies became kings and ruled as a dynasty until the death of Cleopatra in 30 BC, when Egypt came under Roman control. In India, Alexander's empire was taken over by the Mauryans (see Emperor Asoka below).

Meanwhile, at the other end of the Mediterranean, the Phoenicians (see page 41) had set up an empire based on trade.

AMERICAS

500 Large villages of hunters and fishers settle the coasts of Alaska.
400 Olmec civilization in decline.
370 Nazca peoples settle in villages on south coast of Peru.
300 Early Maya period begins. Mayan writing develops and centers for state ceremonies built.
c300 Burial-mound builders in the north-eastern woodlands of North America, Adena and Hopewell peoples.
200 Height of Nazca civilization. Nazca lines cut on a large scale across the desert.
100 Farming settlements of the Mogollon, Hohokam and Anasazi peoples, in the south-west of North America.
100 Okvik hunting people settle in northern Alaska.

⊙ EMPEROR ASOKA OF INDIA

At the end of the 4th century BC, India had its first real emperor, Chandragupta Maurya. His grandson, Asoka, increased the Mauryan Empire and established a road system. Asoka's empire stretched from north of the tributaries of the Rivers Indus and Ganges almost to the southern tip of the continent. Most of the Mauryan population were farmers who paid taxes to the Emperor.

▷ Gate to the Buddhist temple, or *stupa*, at Sanchi in India, built by Asoka.

They did this first in the east Mediterranean then in the west. They were now known as Carthaginians and their new capital was Carthage in North Africa. From here they dominated North Africa and southern Spain.

Rome – world power

No one living around 500 BC could have predicted that the Romans, a small nation calling themselves the Latins, would one day be the most powerful nation on Earth. The Etruscans had established a rich and powerful civilization in Italy yet they were thrown out of Rome itself (see pages 52-3) and many of their ideas and technological advances were claimed by the Romans.

How did the Romans succeed, and for so long (see Timechart page 52) when other civilizations failed? They combined two great strengths. First, they had a trained and professional army which gave them the power to make great conquests. Second, they spread the idea of wanting to be Roman. Of course they made whole nations slaves and could be very cruel, but perhaps no more cruel than many other peoples at that time.

The Great Wall of China

⊙ CH'IN DYNASTY

In 221 BC one man emerged as the most powerful ruler in a period of over 250 years of warfare between cities in China. He was Ch'in Shi-huang-ti. He united the country into an empire and gave China its name. He set up a system of government that lasted until 1912, although his own dynasty was in power for only 11 years. The Emperor Ch'in is probably most famous for building the Great Wall shown here. For centuries the northern states of China had built a number of defences on their boundaries to keep out the 'barbarians'. Ch'in joined all these earthen fortifications together with a huge stone wall. His tomb was found to contain life-size models of 10,000 people.

Merchant caravan on the Silk Road

◉ THE SILK ROAD

Throughout this period there was a great deal of trade between the countries of the Far East, Asia and the Mediterranean. A route known as the Silk Road was established. It was not actually one road but a series of caravan routes between towns and oases. The merchants brought silk from China; but also spices, tortoiseshell, ivory, incense and precious stones from India, Arabia and East Africa were carried on the Silk Road. Slaves and goods such as wine, timber and incense were exported from East Africa.

◉ CELTS AND ROMANS

The Celts, who were known to both the Greeks and the Romans, lived in western Europe from about 700 BC. An excitable warlike people, they invaded Italy in the 5th century and even sacked Rome, the capital city, in 390 BC. In western Europe they lived in defended towns called *oppida* or on defended hilltops (hillforts). Julius Caesar campaigned against them in northern Gaul (modern France) and Britain from 58 to 52 BC.

Rulers of empires

Although there had been empires before 500 BC, they were never as large as those that came after. Each was ruled in a different way but there were similarities. At first the Romans, like the Greeks, had a form of democratic government, but this eventually gave way to the rule of one man, the emperor.

In China there had been years of wars between states although dynasties had ruled there for centuries in the past. One man, Ch'in Shi-huang-ti, became the first true emperor of China in 221 BC. Like the Romans, he established a border around his empire and built strong defences to keep out the 'barbarians'. Asoka ruled in India as an emperor, controlling his vast territory by appointing governors of provinces – just as happened in the Roman and Persian empires (see page 47 and pages 52-3).

A Celtic hillfort under siege

THE ROMAN EMPIRE

The Romans taught their children that the city of Rome was founded by their first king, Romulus, in 753 BC. In fact the name of their city, *Roma*, is an Etruscan word and it was an Etruscan town (see page 43). But it was occupied by various tribes, of which the Latins became the most powerful. They eventually threw out their foreign rulers and established a new kind of state which they called *respublica* – republic.

From republic to empire

For nearly 500 years the Romans were governed by politicians whom they elected by voting. Those elected not only administered the affairs of state but were also in charge of public works, such as road-building, the law courts and the state armies. In the 1st century BC, after several civil wars, Julius Caesar emerged as the most powerful politician in Rome and declared himself dictator. Although Caesar was murdered, his successor Augustus became the ruler of Rome in 31 BC and was later recognized by the people as Emperor.

Ruling the Roman world

Throughout the Roman Empire (see the map below) the people had to be controlled and protected by army units stationed throughout the countryside and along the borders. The Romans were eager to spread their idea of civilization. They built towns with facilities such as public baths and temples and constructed a whole network of roads across their vast empire.

THE ROMAN EMPIRE – RISE AND FALL

753 Legend says Rome was founded by Romulus.
509 Tarquin, the last Etruscan king of Rome, thrown out. Republic founded.
390 Gauls invade Italy and occupy city of Rome.
343-290 Wars with the Samnite people.
264-241 and 218-201 Wars with Carthage.
218 Cathaginian general, Hannibal, crosses Alps and invades Italy.
149-146 Third war with Carthage. Carthage destroyed. North coast of Africa becomes a Roman province.
146 Roman provinces in Greece.
73 Spartacus leads slaves in revolt against Rome.
60 Julius Caesar holds highest political office, the consulship.
59-49 Caesar conquers Gaul and invades Britain twice.
49-45 Civil war. Caesar emerges victorious.
44 (15 March) Julius Caesar assassinated.
27 Augustus declared Emperor.

AD
14 Emperor Augustus dies.
43 Britain invaded and conquered by Emperor Claudius.
64 Great Fire in Rome in the reign of the Emperor Nero.
79 Vesuvius erupts. Roman towns of Pompeii and Herculaneum destroyed.
80 Emperor Titus opens world's largest amphitheatre in Rome, the Colosseum.
122 Emperor Hadrian visits Britain. Hadrian's Wall begun.
212 All men in the Roman provinces made Roman citizens.
267 Goths capture Athens.
312 Christianity declared Rome's official religion.
330 Emperor Constantine moves capital from Rome to Constantinople (later called Byzantium).
455 Rome invaded by Vandals.
475 Romulus Augustulus the last Roman Emperor in the west.
1453 Ottoman Turks capture Constantinople. Fall of the Byzantine Empire.

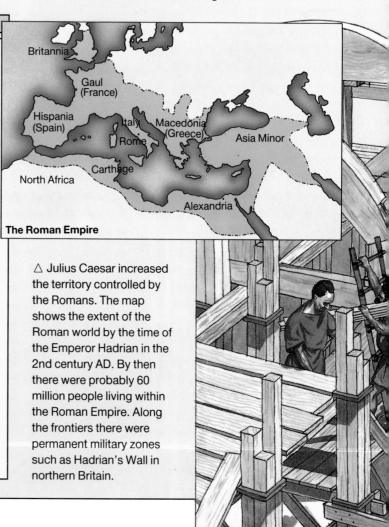

The Roman Empire

Britannia
Gaul (France)
Hispania (Spain)
Italy
Macedonia (Greece)
Rome
Asia Minor
Carthage
North Africa
Alexandria

△ Julius Caesar increased the territory controlled by the Romans. The map shows the extent of the Roman world by the time of the Emperor Hadrian in the 2nd century AD. By then there were probably 60 million people living within the Roman Empire. Along the frontiers there were permanent military zones such as Hadrian's Wall in northern Britain.

Roman soldiers and standard-bearer

◁ The Romans were very good engineers. Here an aqueduct is being built to bring water to a town's houses, industry, public baths and lavatories. Streets were usually laid out on a regular pattern with underground sewerage.

Arches of aqueduct

△ Rome had a paid professional army of about 450,000 men across the Empire. Soldiers were assigned to a 'century' of about 100 men commanded by a centurion. In battle the standard-bearer (on the left) was a rallying point.

53

BARBARIANS AND BATTLES

During the first few centuries AD those civilizations that had established themselves in Europe, Asia and the Far East became more and more sophisticated. But by AD 450 the Western Roman Empire, the Gupta Empire in India and the Han dynasty in China, among others, had all been invaded and destroyed by 'barbarians'.

Barbarians on the borders

The Greeks referred to anyone who in their view was so uncivilized that they could not speak Greek as *barbari* (because they thought

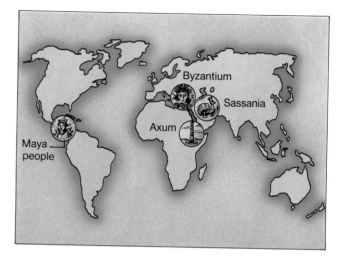

AD 1 – 80	AD 80 – 300	AD 300 – 450
9-23 Hsin replaces the Han dynasty in China. **29** Jesus crucified. **32** Saul converted to Christianity and now called Paul. **43** Romans invade Britain. **60** Kushan Empire established in India. **60** Trial of Paul. **64** Fire destroys Rome. **66** Jewish rebellion against Romans. **67** Paul executed. **73** Jewish stronghold of Masada besieged by Roman army. **79** Vesuvius erupts and destroys Pompeii and Herculaneum.	**80** Colosseum opens in Rome. **100** Kingdom of Axum in Ethiopia established. **100** Paper first used in China. **117** Roman Empire at its greatest extent. **150** Buddhist religion reaches China. **221** China divided into three separate kingdoms. **224** Sassanid dynasty established in Persia. **267** Goths capture Athens. **300** Golden age of Mayan civilization. **304** The Huns cross the Great Wall of China.	**313** Christianity the official Roman religion. **320** Chandragupta I establishes the Gupta dynasty in India. **325** First Council of Christian churches held at Nicaea. **330** Constantine the Great founds new capital at Constantinople. **410** Rome taken by Visigoths. **429** Vandals found kingdom in north Africa. **450** Teotihuacan becomes the sixth-largest city in the world. **475** Last Roman Emperor in the west.

△ In Europe and Asia great civilizations were attacked by 'barbarians'. In Mesoamerica the Maya civilization established itself and flourished.

Jesus on trial

▶ THE TRIAL OF JESUS

Usually the Romans did not try to stop the peoples they conquered worshipping their own gods. But this proved difficult in the case of the Jews and the Christians. The Jews believed that a saviour, called the Messiah, would be sent by God to lead them. Jesus of Nazareth, who was born around 4 BC, was thought by some Jews to be that Messiah. Jesus's followers called him Christ ('the anointed of God'), but many Jews did not believe in him. The Pharisees brought him to trial for blasphemy and handed him over to the Roman governor of Judaea, Pontius Pilate, to carry out the court's sentence of death. In about AD 29 Jesus was crucified. Crucifixion was the normal Roman method of execution for slaves and the lowest criminals.

⊙ THE SIEGE OF MASADA

Opposing Roman rule in Judaea, a group of Jewish resistance fighters took over the mountain fortress rebuilt by King Herod. In AD 73 a Roman army led by the governor of Judaea, Flavius Silva, besieged the fortress. He found that 960 of the Jewish inhabitants had committed suicide.

Romans besiege the Masada fortress

⊙ THE FALL OF ROME

While a separate Eastern Roman Empire had already established itself in Constantinople, the Empire in the west was invaded and occupied by a whole variety of peoples. The north and the east were threatened by the Huns and the Visigoths, who invaded Italy in AD 408. Honorius, the emperor in the Western Empire, failed to hold off the Visigoths, who then installed their own emperor, Attalus. After a disagreement between Attalus and the leader of the Visigoths, Alaric, the Visigoths plundered the city for three days in AD 410. The unthinkable had happened – the capital of the world's most powerful empire, founded over 1,100 years before, had fallen.

The city of Rome under attack

their languages sounded like the baa-ing of sheep!). The Romans used the word for any peoples beyond their borders who threatened their way of life. By the 5th century they included Saxons, who raided the coasts of Britain, and Visigoths, who invaded Italy.

Other civilizations had their own 'barbarians'. The Chinese Empire was threatened by people they called the *Hsiung-nu* – the Huns. In fact, these Huns threatened all the world powers in Europe and Asia. By AD 316 they occupied the northern provinces of China and had begun to settle in the Western Roman Empire by about 370. They destroyed the Gupta Empire in India in about 480, and killed the Sassanian Emperor in 484.

Controlling the long frontiers

To control the territory they claimed as their own, and to keep out invaders, the Chinese authorities had built the Great Wall (see page 50). However, the Romans faced even bigger problems because they had conquered so many lands and had a huge frontier to patrol. By the time of the Emperor Hadrian (AD 117) the Roman Empire stretched from Britain to the Syrian desert, from Germany to North Africa. The Romans too tried building walls for protection, such as Hadrian's Wall (see map page 52) in northern Britain.

Later, they also took other measures to preserve their empire. The Emperor Constantine decided to divide the empire and to found a new capital in the east in AD 330. The Western Empire was overthrown in the 5th century but the Eastern Empire in Asia Minor survived under Byzantine rule until Constantinople fell to the army of the Ottoman Turks in AD 1453.

▼ THE CITY OF CONSTANTINE

Constantinople (the 'city of Constantine') was founded by the Christian emperor Constantine the Great in AD 330 as the capital of the Eastern Roman Empire. It was here that Constantine moved the centre of Roman power and its wealth. This move allowed Roman life, traditions and culture to live on for another thousand years. Constantine's city was laid out with public buildings and squares and the church of Haghia Sophia (below). The Visigoths had been allowed to settle in the Eastern Empire, but the strong wall built around Constantinople in AD 413 kept out these 'barbarians'.

The church of Haghia Sophia

▲ THE MAYA

For 600 years the Maya people of Mesoamerica had developed their own civilization with its cities and ceremonial centres. After about AD 300 this civilization reached its height. Many large cities were built, including Palenque with its palace and observatory shown above. Maya cities were independent states and often at war with each other. They took prisoners whom they sacrificed to their gods. The Maya developed writing based on pictures called 'glyphs'. They also observed the stars and used calendars.

EUROPE

14 Emperor Augustus dies.
43 Roman invasion of Britain under Emperor Claudius.
60 Revolt of eastern Britons against Roman rule, led by Boadicea, Queen of the Iceni.
79 Vesuvius erupts. Pompeii and Herculaneum destroyed.
117 Roman Empire is at its largest under Emperor Trajan.
122 Hadrian's Wall begun.
267 Goths invade Greece and capture Athens.
306 Constantine declared Roman Emperor in York, Britain.
330 Roman Empire capital moves to Constantinople.
409 Vandals and Visigoths invade Europe.
410 Rome taken by Visigoths.
433 Attila leads the Huns.
450 Saxons, Angles and Jutes begin to settle in Britain.
475 Romulus Augustulus, the last Roman Emperor in the west.

AFRICA AND ASIA

60 Kushan Empire established in India.
100 Kingdom of Axum in Ethiopia established.
106 Romans occupy Nabatean kingdom, southern Arabia.
224 Sassanid dynasty established in Persia by Ardashir I.
260 Shapur I from Persia defeats Romans and captures the Emperor Valerian.
320 Chandragupta I founds the Gupta dynasty in India.
325 Axum destroys Kingdom of Meroe in Nubia.
325 First Council of Christian churches at Nicaea (now in Turkey).
330 Founding of Constantinople (now Istanbul, Turkey) by the Roman Emperor Constantine the Great.
400 Kingdom of Axum adopts Christian religion.
429 Vandals invade North Africa and establish a kingdom.

The Romans and religion

At first, the Romans saw Jesus and the early Christians as a threat to their own religion and the Roman way of life. Christians were persecuted and often murdered. However, the Christian message was spread by missionaries like Paul, who journeyed throughout the Mediterranean preaching the Gospel. Many churches were established, and in AD 313 the Emperor Constantine the Great, who was converted to Christianity, made it the official religion of the Romans. The Christian churches, which had been set up all over the Empire, held their first Council in AD 325 at Nicaea, near Constantinople, the capital.

The Romans also had major problems with the Jews living in the land around Jerusalem, before these determined people were eventually overcome. In AD 70 the Jewish temple in Jerusalem was destroyed and the people were forced to scatter in the first of many exiles – called the *diaspora*.

Civilizations in the Americas

While Rome was governing its huge empire, the city of Teotihuacan in Mexico was beginning to extend its influence abroad. By AD 300 the Maya people of Mesoamerica were the most powerful civilization in the area.

▼ AXUM

During the Roman period there were several kingdoms flourishing in east Africa. The Kingdom of Axum was established around AD 100 and was the center of a network of trading routes. Its port of Adulis lies on the Red Sea in modern Ethiopia. Most people in the kingdom were farmers but they also traded in ivory. The tall thin stone below, called a *stela*, which was carved to represent multi-story buildings, stands over an underground tomb.

▼ SASSANIA

Ardashir led a revolt against the Parthians in about AD 224 and became the *shahanshah* – the 'king of kings'. He founded the Sassanian Empire, which eventually stretched from the River Indus to Mesopotamia. Ardashir's son, Shapur I, defeated three Roman emperors and even captured and executed one, Valerian, in about AD 260. Sassanian artwork was particularly fine and attractive, as is shown by the three objects below.

A 68 ft. high stela from Axum

Sassanian objects

FAR EAST

9-23 Wang Mang seizes power in China and establishes Hsin dynasty.
24 Han rulers mount expedition against Wang Mang and re-establish the Han dynasty.
100 First use of paper in China.
150 Buddhist religion reaches China.
220 Later Han dynasty comes to an end.
221 China divided into three separate kingdoms – the Shu, Wei and Wu.
265 General Ssu-ma Yen of the Wei kingdom overcomes the Shu kingdom and becomes the first emperor of the Western Ch'in dynasty.
280 Wu people overcome, now part of Ch'in Empire.
300 Yamato state in Japan controls whole country.
304 Hsiung-nu (Huns) horsemen cross the Great Wall of China.
316 Fall of northern Chinese provinces to the Hun horsemen.
400 Buddhism established in China.

AMERICAS

1 Moche people on north coast of Peru. Basket-making people of south-western North America – hunters and farmers.
150 Rise of the city of Teotihuacan in the Valley of Mexico. Dominates trade in the area. Contact with the Maya.
300 Golden age of the Mayan civilization begins. Large cities. Arts and science flourishes.
300 Zapotec civilization in the highlands of Oaxaca, Mexico.
400 Marajoara people on the Marajo Island at mouth of Amazon river.
450 Trade links between city of Teotihuacan and the Mayans. Teotihuacan sixth-largest city in the world.

TIMECHART 1

TIME PERIODS

The main divisions of prehistory were first defined by 19th-century archaeologists in Europe. The divisions of the STONE AGES, the BRONZE AGE and the IRON AGE were based on the discovery of the different materials used to make tools and weapons. Dates for these periods differ from continent to continent.

THE STONE AGES mark the use of stone of various types to make tools, such as sickles to cut crops, and weapons, for example arrowheads. Both hunting and early farming peoples used stone tools. Other materials were also used – wood, bone, antler horn, leather and so on – but those do not survive as often as stone. In some parts of the world the Stone Ages are defined as:

The Palaeolithic – the Old Stone Age. It is the longest period, dating from the earliest peoples until c10,000 years ago in NW Europe. In N America the Palaeolithic is known as the Palaeo-Indian.

The Mesolithic – the Middle Stone Age. This is the period of the hunter-gatherers in Europe after the last Ice Age.

The Neolithic – the New Stone Age. This is the earliest farming period, when people were still using stone for tools and weapons. In Britain, the Neolithic begins in c4000 BC as farmers using stone tools arrived from mainland Europe.

The Bronze Age starts with the use of copper, sometimes along with stone, for tools and weapons. Copper was being smelted in W Asia and SE Europe by 7000-6000 BC and in E Asia by 2000 BC. Bronze is an alloy of copper and tin and was first used in W Asia by 4000-3000 BC and in China by 2700 BC.

The Iron Age dates from about 2000-1500 BC with the first use of iron in W Asia. Iron was commonly used in Europe by 500 BC and cast iron was produced in China by c500 BC.

AFRICA

4 million First known hominids (Australopithecines) in eastern and southern Africa.
2.5 million First finds of *Homo habilis*.
1.5 million First finds of *Homo erectus*.
100,000 First evidence of modern people *Homo sapiens sapiens* in eastern and southern Africa.
10,000 Hunting camps in Sahara region after last Ice Age.

Australopithecus africanus

8500 First rock art in the Sahara region.
6500 Domesticated cattle in Africa.
6000 Wheat and barley first domesticated in north-eastern Africa.

Saharan rock art 6000 BC

4000 Millet and sorghum cultivated in the Sudan.
3050 Foundation of the Egyptian state.

EUROPE

850,000 Earliest hominids reach Europe from Africa.
600,000 First hand-axes in use.
300,000 Lakeside hunters' settlements in Germany.
120,000 Neanderthal peoples – first humans to bury their dead.
40,000 Last Ice Age.
35,000 First modern humans in Europe.
30,000 First cave art.
8300 Glaciers retreat.
8300 Hunting techniques change and stone tools become smaller and more sophisticated.
6500 First farmers in the Balkans.
6500 Britain separated from mainland Europe by melting of ice.
6200 Farming villages in western Mediterranean.
5200 Farming spreads as far as the Netherlands.

West Kennet long barrow in England, 3600-2500 BC

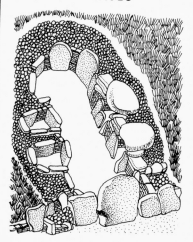

4500 Megalithic tombs in western Europe.
4000 Flint mines.
4000 First farmers in Britain still using stone tools.
3500 Simple plows first used in northern and western Europe.
3200 Circles of megalithic stones in Britain (for example, Stonehenge) and northern France (Carnac).

ASIA

900,000 Earliest hominids in western Asia.
120,000 Neanderthal peoples in western Asia. First discovered burials.
10,000 Natufian settlements in Palestine.
9000 First wheat harvested in Syria. First sheep domesticated in Mesopotamia.
8000 First true farming community at Jericho.

Harvesting wheat 5000 BC

7000 Wheat and barley cultivated in Anatolia. Pig domesticated in Anatolia.
7000 Foundation of Çatal Hüyük, Anatolia.
6000 Farming established in northern Mesopotamia.
5000 Ubaid culture established in Mesopotamia. Irrigation increases farming crops.
4500 Farming established around River Ganges, India.
3650 Earliest vehicle burials in the world in southern Russia.
3500 First civilization based on cities established in Sumeria.
3250 Earliest writing in the world, in Mesopotamia, in the form of pictographic clay tablets.
3100 Cuneiform writing used in Mesopotamia. Long-distance trade with Syria.

AMERICAS

30,000 Earliest evidence for humans, Brazil.
13,000 Earliest human evidence in Alaska.

Fulsom point stone axe 9000 BC

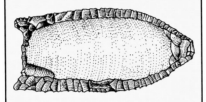

12,000 Earliest human evidence in North America.
10,000 People reach southern tip of Americas.
Ice sheets melt in North America, more temporary settlements of hunters.
8500 First cultivation of wild grasses and beans in Peru.
8000 Archaic period in North America. New types of stone tools. First burials. Many large game animals extinct.
7000 First crops cultivated in Mexico. Some semi-permanent farming settlements in North America.
6300 Grain and potato cultivation in Peru.
5000 Cultivation of maize in Mexico. Small-scale cultivation in Amazon region.
4000-3000 Inuits (Eskimos) moved from Asia into America.

Cotton textile, Peru 2000 BC

3500 Llama used as pack animal in Peru. Cotton cultivated and textiles made in Peru.
3200 Maize cultivated in South America.

CHINA AND AUSTRALASIA

450,000 Earliest evidence for humans in China.
120,000 *Homo sapiens* type in Java.
90,000 First hominids in East Asia.
40,000 First human settlers in Australia.
25,000 Many settlements of hunters in Australia. First settlers arrive in New Guinea and Tasmania.

Japanese pot 9000 BC

10,500 Earliest pottery in the world in Japan.
8000 End of Ice Age. More islands created in South-East Asia.
7000 First cultivation of root crops in New Guinea.
6000 First farming villages in China. Agriculture spreads to South-East Asia.

Chinese village 3000 BC

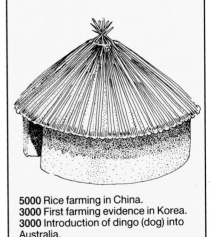

5000 Rice farming in China.
3000 First farming evidence in Korea.
3000 Introduction of dingo (dog) into Australia.

DATE SYSTEMS

Different peoples used different ways of writing dates. In Mesopotamia lists of kings give the dates of important events. From Ancient Egypt lists of kings in chronological order have survived. So have some of the inscriptions cut on the walls of temples in Egypt.

The word *calendar* comes from the Latin meaning the first day of the month. Different peoples reckoned their dating systems from a particular happening. For example, the Jewish calendar dates from the supposed creation of the world in 3761 BC.

The Maya people in ancient America used a system of dates which we can decipher today. Their calendar starts at our equivalent of 3114 BC.The Romans used the lists of their elected consuls to date events, and later their emperors.

In the Timecharts here and on pages 58-59, dates are given as either **BC** or **AD**. **BC** means 'Before Christ' and is based on the supposed date of the birth of Christ (see page 54). Dates are counted backwards in this period. So, Tuthankamon was buried in 1323 BC, which was before Augustus became Rome's first emperor in 27 BC.

AD stands for *Anno Domini* which is Latin for 'in the year of the Lord'. Dates work forwards from this period. Christ was crucified in AD 29. By AD 450 the city of Teotihuacan is the sixth-largest in the world. The world's first astronaut walked on the Moon in 1969 (or AD 1969). Today dates are usually given without the letters AD.

C stands for *circa* which is Latin for 'about'. It is used with dates that we do not know precisely.

The Romans began their dating system from the foundations of the city of Rome in 753 BC. Their calendar was reorganized by Julius Ceasar in 46 BC into years of 365 days with an extra day every four years (our Leap Year). The Julian Calendar, as it was known, was used until 1582 when Pope Gregory modified it slightly. All Roman Catholic countries adopted this new Gregorian Calendar immediately. Britain changed to the Gregorian Calendar in 1752 and Russia in 1917.

AFRICA

3000 Egyptian hieroglyphic writing.
2630 First pyramid begun.
2530 Great Pyramid at Giza built.
2500 Sahara begins to dry out.
2040 Egypt reunited and ruled from Thebes.
1652 War between Egypt and the Hyksos peoples from Asia.
1367 New Egyptian king adopts the name Akhenaten and breaks with established religion.
1323 King Tuthankhamon of Egypt is buried.
1218 and 1182 Invasion of Egypt by the Sea Peoples.

Tuthankhamon's coffin 1323 BC

900 Foundation of the Kingdom of Kush.
814 Phoenicians found new city of Carthage, North Africa.
800 Beginnings of the Nok culture.
671 Assyrians conquer Egypt.
600 Phoenicians sail around Africa.
450 Ironworking methods reach the Nok culture from Carthage.
146 Carthage destroyed by Rome.
30 Egypt becomes a Roman province.

AD
100 Kingdom of Axum in Ethiopia established.
325 Axum destroys Kingdom of Meroe in Nubia.
400 Kingdom of Axum adopts Christian religion.
429 Vandals invade north Africa and establish a kingdom.

EUROPE

2600 Early Minoan period in Crete begins.
1700 New palaces built on Crete.
1500 Mycenaean civilization established.
1450 Eruption at Thera. End of Minoan civilization.
1200 Mycenaeans under threat from Sea Peoples.
1150 Mycenae destroyed.
850-750 Epic poet Homer may have lived at this time.
776 First Olympic Games held.
753 Traditional date for founding of Rome.
700 Scythians build fortified settlements in eastern Europe.
508 Democratic government in Athens.
490 Greeks beat off Persian invasion at the Battle of Marathon.
447 Building of the Parthenon begins.
390 Gauls occupy city of Rome.
334 Alexander the Great's campaigns against the Persians.
300 Celtic states formed in Europe.
250 All Italy controlled by Romans.
218 Hannibal crosses Alps into Italy.
146 Greece occupied by the Romans.
100 Celts develop defended settlements – *oppida*.
59-49 Gaul conquered by the Romans.

Bust of Julius Caesar c50 BC

44 Julius Caesar assassinated.
27 Augustus, first Roman emperor.
4 Jesus born.

AD
29 Jesus Christ crucified.
79 Vesuvius erupts. Pompeii and Herculaneam destroyed.
117 Roman Empire at its greatest.
267 Goths capture Athens.
313 Christianity adopted as the official Roman religion.
330 Roman capital moved to Constantinople.
376 Visigoths cross River Danube.
410 Rome taken by Visigoths.
433 Attila leads the Huns.
450 Saxons, Angles and Jutes settle in Britain.

ASIA

2500 City states such as Ur in Mesopotamia.
2500 First cities established in Indus Valley, India.
2000 Amorite dynasty in Babylonia. **Hittites** invade Anatolia.
1900 Indus Valley civilization in decline.
1800 Assyrians invade northern Babylonia. Assyrian Empire.
1792 Hammurapi reigns in Babylon.
1250 Israelite tribes move from Egypt to Israel.
1200 Hittite Empire collapses.

Babylonian cuneiform c1700 BC

1000 Kingdom of Israel under King David.
883 Further Assyrians conquests.
627 Assyrian Empire at its largest.
604 Nebuchadnezzar II rules Babylonian Empire.
539 Babylonia conquered by Persians.
522 Darius I rules Persian Empire.
482 Persian ruler, Xerxes, crushes revolt in Babylon.
333 Alexander the Great defeats Persians at Battle of Issos.
327 Alexander the Great in India.
321 Chandragupta founds Mauryan Empire in India.
270 Asoka takes over the Mauryan throne.
240 Parthian dynasty begins in northern Persia.
53 Parthia stops Roman expansion east.

AD
60 Kushan Empire established in India.
224 Sassanid dynasty in Persia.
320 Gupta dynasty founded in India.
325 First Council of Christian churches held at Nicaea.

AMERICAS

2500 First large settlements with temple mounds in Andes region. Long-distance trade.
2300 Settlements in Mesoamerica.
2000 Maize cultivated on a large scale in the Andes region.
2000 Inuits (Eskimos) reach northern part of Greenland.
1200 First civilizations in Mesoamerica based on cities. Beginnings of the Olmec civilization.
1000 Eastern woodlands peoples of North America, settlements and rich burials.
Dorset hunting people spread across the Arctic.
900 Chavin civilization in the Andes. Oldest known Olmec center in Mesoamerica destroyed.
800 Zapotec civilization in Mesoamerica produces first writing in the Americas.
400 Olmec civilization in decline.

Nazca land markings c300 BC

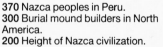

370 Nazca peoples in Peru.
300 Burial mound builders in North America.
200 Height of Nazca civilization.
100 Okvik hunters in northern Alaska.

AD
150 Rise of the city of Teotihuacan in the Valley of Mexico.
300 Golden age of Mayan civilization begins.
450 Teotihuacan sixth-largest city in the world. Links with Mayans.

CHINA AND AUSTRALASIA

3000 Society evolving in China. Use of stone tools.
2500 First domesticated animals on islands in South-East Asia.
2500 First wheel-thrown pottery in China.
2205 China's first emperor, Yu. Metalworking introduced.
2000 Agriculture in New Guinea.
1600 Beginning of the Shang dynasty in China.
1400 Chinese capital moved to Anyang. Rich burial of kings and nobles, with chariots, horses and drivers.
1027 Last Shang king overthrown.
1000 Peoples reach almost every island in Polynesia.
1000 Long-distance trade across Australia.
500 Cast iron first used in China. First Chinese coins.

Great Wall of China c200 BC

481 Central authority in China breaks down.
479 Chinese philosopher Confucius dies.
221 China reunited.
214 Great Wall of China begun.
207 Han dynasty in China begins.

AD
24 Han dynasty re-established after period of war.
100 Paper first used in China.
150 Buddhism reaches China.
221 China divided into three kingdoms.
265 Central control in China in the Western Chin dynasty.
304 Huns cross the Great Wall.

GLOSSARY

acropolis The highest point in a Greek town; usually defended.

AD The abbreviated form of 'anno domini' used for dates (see page 60).

agricultural revolution The change that came about when people learned to survive by growing food and breeding animals instead of by hunting and gathering food.

aqueduct A channel to bring water into a town, sometimes carried over valleys by a series of arches.

archaeologist A scientist who collects and interprets evidence from the past which survives under or on the ground.

BC The abbreviated form of 'Before Christ' used for dates (see page 60).

burial mound A mound, usually of earth, heaped over the buried remains of a person to form an impressive monument.

citizen A person (usually male in ancient societies) who had rights of voting in cities.

city-state A city with enough independence to control a territory around it. City-states often linked together as countries.

civilization An organized society with its own identity, sufficiently wealthy to have influence over a large territory.

colony A settlement of people establishing their way of life outside their own country.

cultivate To work the land to produce crops.

cuneiform A form of writing, invented by the Sumerians, in which wedge shapes are pushed into clay.

democracy A form of government, invented by the Greeks, where citizens vote for their own officials.

domesticate To breed animals from the wild and tame them over generations, often for the meat or milk that they produce.

dynasty The ruling family of a king or emperor in which power passes from one generation to another.

empire A large territory ruled over by an emperor or a king and extending far beyond the ruler's homeland.

Fertile Crescent The lands from the Red Sea to the Persian Gulf which form roughly a crescent shape. There farming first developed.

frontier A boundary of a territory or empire, often defended by forts.

hieroglyph(ic) A form of writing, used in Ancient Egypt, in which drawings indicate words, letters or syllables.

hominid An early form of human.

inscription Writing cut into stone or metal, for official purposes.

irrigation An organized form of watering fields and crops by cutting channels from a water source.

megalith A large stone monument like the prehistoric stone circles.

Mesoamerica The area of land between North and South America (from Mexico to Panama).

migration The movement of peoples to new lands.

mummification A process used by the Egyptians and others for preserving a body after death.

nomads People whose way of life keeps them moving across their territory without making permanent **settlements**.

oppida Fortified settlements of the Celtic people in northern Europe.

papyrus A form of writing 'paper' made from the flattened leaves of river reeds.

Pharaoh The title for an Egyptian king from about 1350 BC, meaning 'the Great House'.

pictogram The earliest form of writing using pictures.

prehistory The period before the invention of written records.

province A conquered land governed as part of an **empire**.

pyramid A tomb for an Egyptian king; it is called after its shape.

scribe A writer of official documents.

settlement A place where people live and build a group of houses together.

steppes Russian name for huge areas of grassland plains.

vizier The highest-grade official in the Egyptian government.

ziggurat A temple tower found first in Sumeria.

INDEX

Peter Bedrick Books of Related Interest

**What Do We Know About
the Egyptians?**
Joanna Defrates, 100+ full color illus.,
40 pages, 8½ x 11,
ISBN 0-87226-353-3

**What Do We Know About
the Romans?**
Mike Corbishley, 100+ full color illus.,
40 pages, 8½ x 11,
ISBN 0-87226-352-5

**Gods & Pharoahs from
Egyptian Mythology**
Geraldine Harris, 18 full color illus.,
43 line drawings, 132 pages, 8½ x 11,
ISBN 0-87226-907-8

**Illustrated Dictionary of
Greek & Roman Mythology**
Michael Stapleton, 64 b&w illus.,
244 pages, 6 x 9 ISBN 0-87226-200-6, pb
ISBN 0-87226-063-1, hc

**Heroes, Gods & Emperors
from Roman Mythology**
Kerry Usher, 18 full color illus.,
46 line drawings, 132 pages,
8½ x 11, ISBN 0-87226-909-4

**Gods, Men & Monsters
from the Greek Myths**
Michael Gibson, 23 full color illus.,
50 line drawings, 132 pages,
8½ x 11, ISBN 0-87226-911-6

First Civilizations
Giovanni Caselli, full color illus.,
48 pages, 8½ x 11,
ISBN 0-91745-59-9

Everyday Life of Series

An Ice Age Hunter
ISBN 0-87226-103-4

An Egyptian Craftsman
ISBN 0-87226-100-X

A Greek Potter
ISBN 0-87226-101-8

A Roman Soldier
ISBN 0-87226-106-9

Full color illustrations throughout,
32 pages, 7½ x 101/4